WORDPRESS FOR WRITERS

CREATE AN AWESOME AUTHOR WEBSITE THAT HELPS YOU SELL BOOKS

RACHEL MCCOLLIN

CONTENTS

Part X
OVER TO YOU

I

INTRODUCTION

1

BEFORE WE BEGIN

WELCOME to this book on author websites.

Author websites, you might be thinking. *What a dull subject.*

Well… yup. It can be pretty dull. After all, you're a writer. You want to spend your time writing, not tinkering about with web pages, and blog posts, and code.

But wait right up. (Did you hear the needle-dragging-on-vinyl sound effect that I did there, or am I just showing my age?)

Websites don't have to be dull.

They don't have to be difficult.

And they don't have to be expensive.

If you're a writer who is serious about their career and knows they need an online presence, chances are that at some point, someone has tried to convince you that you can only get a decent author website if you fork out a ton of cash or devote your evenings to learning code.

This book is here to dispel that myth.

I've been creating websites with WordPress since 2010, and I know that it isn't as hard as some people want you to think.

It also isn't as expensive.

And this book will show you how.

I'm going to do my level best to make what you're about to read straightforward, instructive, and entertaining.

So come along with me for the ride, and get yourself an awesome author website without breaking the bank, and without writing a line of code.

WHAT THIS BOOK WILL TEACH YOU

Let's keep this simple.

This book will teach you one thing: how to create your author website using WordPress.

It won't teach you code.

It won't teach you about website builders (although if you want to know more about that, you might like my free book *Author Website Blueprint*).

It won't teach you how to use social media.

And it won't teach you how to set up a mailing list (although it will teach you how to use your website to get signups).

Once you've read this book, you'll have everything you need to create yourself a professional, easy-to-maintain author website with WordPress.

I'll show you how WordPress.com works, as well as self-hosted WordPress (or WordPress.org). If you don't know what those two things are, I'll show you the difference, and help you decide between them.

I'll teach you how to use free plugins and themes to get your website humming and make it work for you.

I'll teach you how to find hosting for your site and how to keep costs down.

And I'll teach you how to use your website to engage with your readers, build a loyal following of fans, and ultimately sell books.

That sounds like a grand promise, right? Well, yeah, it is. I can't promise you that having a professional author website will sell you books.

But I can tell you it'll increase your chances.

So, here's what you're going to learn in more detail:

- The difference between WordPress.com and self-hosted WordPress, and how to choose between them.
- How to get hosting for a self-hosted site or sign up for a WordPress.com site.
- How to create your site and link it to your domain name.
- How to choose and customize a theme so your site reflects your author brand.
- How to install and activate plugins that will make your site secure, fast, and easily searched by Google.
- How to create content for your site, including tips on what and when to publish.
- How to hook your website up with your mailing list and use it to get newsletter signups.

Here are the things you're not going to learn:

- How to write code.
- How to hire an expensive web designer to do something you could easily do yourself.
- How to create a crappy website that looks like you built it for free.
- How to use cat memes to make your writing go viral and propel you to superstardom (sorry).

The first two of those are things you've probably been told you need to do if you want a self-hosted WordPress site. I'm going to say it again, and for the last time: you **don't** need to do those things.

The third is something you might be worried about if you have a low budget and no experience with websites. This book will help you create a site that doesn't look home-made and doesn't look free.

And the fourth—well, if I crack that, I'm hardly going to share my secrets, am I?

WHO AM I TO TELL YOU ABOUT WORDPRESS AUTHOR WEBSITES?

So, I've already told you that some of the myths surrounding Word-Press are wrong.

But who am I to say that?

Here's a little bit about me and my relevant experience (feel free to skip this if you really couldn't care).

I've been creating websites since 2001. I started out writing HTML, then learned CSS (you don't need to know what these are), and then in 2010 I stumbled upon WordPress.

WordPress is what's called a content management system, or CMS. It lets you add content to a website and create new pages without writing code.

At that time, I'd just set up a new web design business, and clients were crying out for sites they could update themselves, without writing code (are you sensing a theme here?).

WordPress was the answer.

I wasted no time in learning WordPress inside and out, coding my own themes and plugins and developing a bunch of client sites built on WordPress.

This was around the time that mobile websites became huge, so I threw myself into learning about that. I immersed myself in something called responsive web design, which is how you make a website resize itself so it looks great on all screen sizes.

I was lucky: this was a brand-new field and being new to the industry gave me an advantage. I built up a reputation and was approached by a publisher to write a book on the subject.

That book was *WordPress Mobile Web Development* (catchy title, I know). Please don't go and seek it out on Amazon—it is still for sale but it was published so long ago that it's probably way out of date. Scrub that, it *is* out of date. But amazingly, it still sells a few copies.

That led to three more WordPress books and a boatload of tutorials, articles, courses and blog posts for some of the biggest Word-Press sources out there.

My career started to shift from being a WordPress developer to being a WordPress teacher and writer. I've written hundreds of guides to aspects of WordPress, for everyone from complete beginners to advanced professionals.

I hope I've convinced you that I know about WordPress. But what about how it applies to writers?

After writing my four books on WordPress, I was inspired to pursue something I'd always wanted to do—write fiction. I chose to become an indie publisher, setting up my own small imprint and doing my own publishing and marketing, as well as hiring professionals like editors and cover designers.

To support all this, I developed a website (three actually, as I have three pen names). So, I set about learning how to use Word-Press to support an author career.

At writing conferences and events, I often find myself giving out advice on author websites. And last year at one of these events, someone said to me, 'Why don't you write a book on WordPress, for writers?'

This, dear reader, is the result of that conversation. I hope to give you the benefit of my experience with websites in general, and WordPress in particular, to make the whole thing easier for you.

Anyway, in case you skipped this bit, here's the TL;DR version. I've been a WordPress developer and teacher since 2010, and I'm a writer. So, I like to think I've got a decent amount of experience in this area.

WHO THIS BOOK IS FOR

This book is for all writers, at all stages of their careers, and using all publishing models.

Instead of focusing on what kind of writer you might be, and whether you fit on a list of my ideal readers, I'm going to ask you two questions:

1. Do you want to reach more readers?
2. Do you want to use a website to help you with that?

If the answer to both of those questions is yes, then this book is for you.

If you already have a website, or even if you've never considered setting one up, you'll find this book useful.

WHO THIS BOOK IS NOT FOR

What? you're thinking. *Why is she trying to put people off reading her book?*

Well, all books have a target audience, and I want everyone who reads this book to benefit from it.

So here are a couple more questions:

1. Do you have no time to spend creating your author website and would rather throw money at someone else so they can do it?
2. Are you content to have a crappy author website that looks like it was created in 1993?

If the answer to either of these questions is yes, then this isn't the book for you.

I'm going to show you how to create a modern, professional website, and I'm going to show you how to do it yourself, either for free or for minimal cost (a few dollars a month).

You will need some time—but not loads. Maybe a weekend, or a week's worth of evenings. But some.

You won't need a lot of technical skills. If you've got the skills to set up a professional-looking Facebook page, you'll be fine setting up a WordPress website. I'm not saying the process is the same, just that the level of technical ability is similar.

If you do plan to hire someone else to create your website but will manage it yourself, you might find the later chapters useful as they'll help you with content. So, maybe it's just the people who want crappy websites that this book won't help.

Unless you're a fan of Ling's Cars (wp4writers.com/ling), one of the most notoriously vile websites on the internet. The owner has been claiming for years that this site gets her a shedload of business (maybe because it's so infamous?).

Image 1-1 The Ling's cars website

In that case, go ahead and get yourself a really nasty website.

HOW TO USE THIS BOOK

This book is designed to be used in one of two ways:

- Follow it through in order, using the steps here to create your author website from scratch.
- Dip in and out and use the bits you need as and when you need them.

Or a combination of the two!

It really doesn't matter how you use the book. I've written it so that you don't have to read Chapter Two to make sense of Chapter Six, for example. But if you are new to this topic, I do recommend you start with Chapter One, so you know what WordPress is and why I'm recommending it.

If you've already got an author website but need to spruce it up a bit, or make it run more smoothly, then you may find that dipping into some of the later chapters works better for you.

It's up to you.

JARGON BUSTER

Any book about websites is bound to contain some jargon. It's impossible to avoid without getting too wordy. So, where necessary, I've added asides to this book explaining technical terms.

They look like this:

Helpful text
Here's an explanation of some jargon you might have come across in the text.

There's also a jargon buster at the back of the book which you can refer to as you read the book or while you're working on your website.

EXTRA RESOURCES

Throughout this book, I'm going to be guiding you through some processes. In the paperback version of the book, there will be screenshots so you can see exactly what you should be looking at.

In the e-book version of the book, it's difficult to get screenshots to display nicely without messing up the rest of the book. It also makes the book more expensive, due to file size. So instead of forcing you to try and look at detailed images on your Kindle, I've created a section of my website that you can access, with all the screenshots. I'll give them each a unique reference, which will be in the book and on the website.

You can find all this at wp4writers.com/resources.

Here you'll also find a constantly growing list of blog posts and resources that will give you more in-depth knowledge and help you apply what you've learned in this book. I add to this every week, so keep going back.

And if you want to get an update when there's a new blog post (and get a copy of my free book *Author Website Blueprint*), you can sign up for my VIP Club at wp4writers.com/club.

II

WHY WORDPRESS?

2

BENEFITS OF WORDPRESS

This book is about creating an author website with WordPress. It doesn't cover website builders, or blogging platforms, or any other way of creating a website.

I made that decision deliberately. Partly because if the book covered everything, it would be way too long, but mainly because I believe WordPress is easily the best platform for a professional author website.

WHY WORDPRESS?

Throughout this book, I'm assuming that you want an author website because you want something that reflects well on you and your books. In other words, you want a professional website.

WordPress is the website platform used by over a quarter of the entire internet. It's used by everyone from mom and pop operations to multinational conglomerates, because it's flexible, robust, and great value for money.

Here are a few reasons why I think WordPress rocks.

1. IT'S FREE OR VERY CHEAP

The code underpinning WordPress is free, and always will be.

You might be rolling your eyes and saying, *yeah, yeah, I've heard that before. Facebook told me that reaching my fans would be free, but now I have to pay to boost posts.*

WordPress is different from Facebook. Facebook is and always has been a for-profit business. WordPress is run by a nonprofit organization called the WordPress Foundation. Its code is developed by hundreds if not thousands of volunteers. Some of these people are paid for their time, yes, but they're not paid by the WordPress Foundation. They're paid by the companies that employ them, because these companies are built around Word-Press and know that developing WordPress is good for their business.

This is a model called Open Source. WordPress isn't the only software built on this model: if you want to find out more about it, check out the Wikipedia article at wp4writers.com/opensource.

Now, in the real world, if you want a professional website you're going to have to pay something. If your site is built on self-hosted WordPress, you'll have to buy hosting. If you're on WordPress.com and want advanced features (such as your own domain name), you'll need to pay for a premium plan.

But neither of these will cost you a lot of money.

2. IT'S POPULAR

So what? you ask. *I don't want to follow the crowd.*

But using software that's popular gives you two advantages:

- It's less likely to disappear.
- If you need help, there's plenty available.

The WordPress support forums are packed with helpful people who are happy to answer your questions. There are thousands if not millions of articles on the internet which will answer your Word-

Press questions. And if you do need to hire a developer in the future, you'll have no problem finding one.

Using the world's biggest content management system (CMS) gives you a degree of security that many other platforms can't give you.

Whoah, hang on a minute, what's a CMS again?

A CMS, or content management system, is software that creates a website to which you can add content without coding new pages. It has admin screens for you to create and edit that content, then stores it in a database. The software then pulls all this together when people visit your site, to create the pages on your site.

---

3. IT'S ON YOUR TURF

This third benefit only applies to self-hosted WordPress sites.

You may have heard it said that your author newsletter is important because it's yours. Unlike your Facebook fans, or your Twitter followers, it's *your* list. You have access to the data, can use it to keep in touch with people, and can keep it even if your mailing list provider goes under.

A self-hosted WordPress site is similar. Unlike a site on a website builder like Wix or a blogging platform like Blogger, it's yours. You own the code files and all of the content. Sure, you'll need to buy hosting space to host that code and content on, but your hosting provider has no rights to your website.

If your hosting provider should go out of business (or if you decide they aren't good enough anymore), you can take all of your code and your content and move it to another hosting provider. A good hosting provider will do all this for you when you move to them. But if Wix disappeared and you decided to move to Square-Space (i.e. from one website builder to another), you'd have to start again from scratch.

4. IT'S FLEXIBLE

WordPress is by far the most flexible website platform. By installing plugins in a self-hosted site, you can add just about whatever you like to it.

Plugins? What are they? I'm not an electrician.

A plugin is extra code that makes something happen on your site. It might add a link to your newsletter provider, or an online store, or a gallery of cute cat photos. It means that the core code for WordPress itself doesn't have to include stuff you might not need. If you want that extra functionality, just install a plugin.

Installing plugins is easy and you can do it from the WordPress admin screens. I'll cover it in Chapter 15.

Want a video streaming site? WordPress can do it.

Want to sell books in your own online store? No problem, and for free.

Want to add an extra section, for books, or events, or worlds, or anything?

Want to add maps, or quizzes, or slideshows?

Want to give up writing and turn your site into a hub for your favorite cat memes? WordPress has your back, you lucky thing.

WordPress can run anything from a one-page site designed to just get mailing list signups, to a vast multimedia site with everything you could ever want to tell readers about your world-building and characters. And you can add whatever you want as you go along, without deciding on all of it at the beginning.

Start small, and grow—if you need to.

And even better, you can do it all without spending any extra money.

5. IT'S ROBUST

Some years ago, WordPress had a reputation for being insecure. This was largely because of one specific plugin that introduced vulnerabilities to the system, and that was by no means installed on every WordPress site.

Since then, things have changed. WordPress is secure, it's fast, it's well-coded, it's accessible, it's mobile-friendly (with the right theme), and it's easy to back up.

If this weren't the case, then news sites and government bodies wouldn't use it. And they do.

WordPress is based on clean, well-written code that means your site will run faster, something Google loves (other search engines are available). A fast site will boost your search engine rankings.

With the addition of some free plugins, you can make a self-hosted WordPress site more robust still, enhancing security, boosting speed, and making it easy to back up and restore your site with one click. With WordPress.com, this all comes out-of-the-box.

As long as you keep your site up to date (which can be automated), you can have peace of mind.

6. IT'S USER-FRIENDLY

Why have I left this till last?

Because it's one of those myths about WordPress. It has a reputation for being unwieldy and hard to work with.

It's a myth that's sometimes spread by people who've worked with WordPress in a corporate environment; people whose employers probably have a highly-customized site that may be less than intuitive. A site like this is worlds away from the kind of WordPress site an author needs.

With the right theme, you can get yourself set up with a gorgeous site using an interface that's as easy to learn as many website builders.

The new interface for writing posts is designed to be user-friendly and intuitive, with a full-screen mode that lets you focus on your writing, and blocks to help you add media and other types of content.

Installing and activating plugins is all done via the admin screens (no code required).

Now, I'm not going to say that WordPress is as intuitive as every website builder. But I believe that the trade-offs for that aren't worth it. Website builders give you less flexibility, can run slower, aren't as accessible for people with disabilities, and can be much, much more expensive.

This book will help you learn how WordPress works and get to grips with the admin screens. So you won't have to struggle. With this book on your desk, and a few hours to explore, you'll be like the millions of others who are comfortable using WordPress.

WHAT'S THE COMPETITION?

Before we leave this subject, let's take a quick look at the other options available to you, and how they compare.

WEBSITE BUILDERS

Website builders include systems like Wix and SquareSpace. They pride themselves in being intuitive and user-friendly.

I'm not denying that they can be. But they lack the flexibility of WordPress (most of them won't connect to your mailing list provider, for example) and can be expensive.

If you want to expand your WordPress site over time, you can. For free. If you want to add a store, or extra domain names, or multiple sites for multiple pen names, it won't cost you any extra. But with a website builder, it most probably will.

For a more detailed look at website builders and what they offer, you might want to read my free book *Author Website Blueprint*, which you can download from my website at rachelmcwrites.com/blueprint.

BLOGGING PLATFORMS

Blogging platforms include Blogger and Tumblr. In fact, WordPress started out as a blogging platform but quickly grew.

Blogging platforms are OK if you just want to blog in your spare time. They're great for hobbyists, and people who just want to communicate with fellow enthusiasts on their subject.

But most of them haven't updated their design options for many years, or at least if they have, you wouldn't know it. They'll often have banners advertising the blogging platform. They aren't easy to extend. They don't link to your mailing list provider.

In short, blogging platforms are not suitable for any kind of professional website. That's why WordPress evolved from a blogging platform to a CMS. It can still be used for blogs, but it can also be used professionally.

Right at the beginning of this book (not that long ago), I made the assumption that you want a website to support your author career. That means you need a professional website.

I don't believe a blogging platform will give you that.

But if you still aren't convinced, and want to know more, read my free *Author Website Blueprint*.

3

WORDPRESS.COM VS WORDPRESS.ORG

So, now for the million-dollar question.

Should you get yourself a WordPress.com site or a self-hosted (WordPress.org) one?

It's a good question, and one I see debated on author forums. To choose, you need to know the difference. This chapter will enlighten you.

HELP! I'M CONFUSED

First up, let's identify what the difference is between WordPress.com and WordPress.org. I'm going to start with WordPress.org, as that's where it all started.

WORDPRESS.ORG

WordPress.org, also known as self-hosted WordPress, is a set of code that creates a website for you. To get your own website, you install that code on your hosting account, and then set up your website.

Stop! What's this hosting you keep talking about?

Hosting is space on the Internet where you host your website. Having a hosting account means you're hiring some space from a company called a hosting provider, where the code for your website will live. They run servers which store the code.

This isn't free (after all, the hosting provider has to provide the hardware, maintain it and keep it running) but shouldn't cost more than a few dollars a month. Find out which hosting providers I recommend at wp4writers.com/hosting.

The code is open source, and anyone can download it for free. You can either download it from the WordPress.org website (wp4writers.com/wpdownload), or you can use a one-click auto installer provided by your hosting company (which is much easier). I'll show you how to do this later in this book.

Once you've done that, you can do whatever you like with the code—it's yours. You can add a theme to define the way the site looks. You can add plugins to give your site extra functionality like mailing list signups or a social media feed. You can even add your own code if you want, or edit the existing code (not a good idea if you're not experienced).

There are thousands of free plugins and themes (themes are the code that defines how your site looks). If you like, you can pay for a premium theme or plugin. You don't get these from WordPress, but from a third-party provider. I don't believe you need a premium theme to create a professional author website.

So to sum up, with a WordPress.org site, you buy hosting and then install the free software and add whatever theme or plugins you want. If you don't buy premium themes or plugins, all you pay for is the hosting.

WORDPRESS.COM

WordPress.com is a huge installation of WordPress that belongs to a commercial provider. This isn't the same organization that runs WordPress overall—that's a nonprofit foundation.

This provider (its name is Automattic) lets you create a site on their server, meaning the code belongs to them. You can get a basic site for free, but if you want extra features such as a better-than-average theme, getting rid of ads or to use your own domain, you'll have to pay.

There are two main differences:

- The code isn't yours. If the site goes down, or WordPress.com ceases to exist (admittedly unlikely), your site is lost.
- You're limited to the themes and plugins offered by WordPress.com. You can't add any others unless you pay for a top-end plan.

The upside is that if you're starting out on a tight budget, you can get a free site, then build on that in future when funds allow. But for a professional author site, I would recommend no adverts and your own domain—neither of which comes with the free plan.

If you decide to switch from WordPress.com to self-hosted WordPress further down the line, you can—and I'll show you how in this book.

So now let's take a look at the pros and cons of the two platforms.

WORDPRESS.COM—YOUR SITE, THEIR REAL ESTATE

WordPress.com is often seen as an entry-level way of getting yourself a website. If you're just trying WordPress out, it can be a good way to do so without committing yourself. Let's take a look at some of the pros and cons.

THE GOOD

- Free to start.
- Support forums and help are good.
- Easy to set up—just sign up for an account and you're good to go.
- Social media features included such as social sharing and social media buttons.
- You become part of the WordPress.com community and can follow other bloggers (and encourage them to follow you).
- If there are technical problems, you don't have to fix them.
- If you decide to switch to self-hosted WordPress in future, the export/import tool lets you copy all of your content across (but not your theme, plugins or settings).

THE BAD

- Limited choice of themes and plugins.
- The only mailing list provider it'll link to is MailChimp.
- Your website is not yours.

THE UGLY

- A free plan will give you a domain like *authorame.wordpress.com*, which is not as professional as *authorname.com*. You'll have to pay extra to unlock your own domain name.
- A free plan means adverts on your site. You have no way

of controlling what the ads are for and what they look like. For me, this is the biggest downside to a free plan.

WORDPRESS.ORG—YOUR SITE ON YOUR OWN REAL ESTATE

WordPress.org will give you more flexibility and could end up costing you less. To my mind, it's the best tool for a professional website.

THE GOOD

- Once you've installed the software, the site is all yours.
- Thousands of free themes and plugins to choose from.
- Easy to extend and adapt.
- Use your own domain name—many hosting providers will give you one free with your hosting.
- If your hosting provider has an auto-installer, can be installed with just a click of a button.
- No adverts unless you want to monetize your site and install an advertising plugin, in which case you have control.
- Support forums and resources available all over the internet to help you.
- If you like the WordPress.com features, you can add those to a WordPress.org site with the free Jetpack plugin.

THE BAD

- You have to find a hosting provider (I give some tips on that later in this book).

- You have to install the software, even if that is just one-click.
- Thousands of free themes and plugins mean you can be overwhelmed by choice (again, I'll try to help with that here).

THE UGLY

- If your site goes down, you'll have to contact your hosting provider and get them to fix it. Some hosting providers' support is better than others.
- If you install a plugin that breaks your site, you'll have to uninstall it.
- If your site is attacked, you'll be responsible for restoring a clean version (although your hosting provider may well help you and you can install a plugin to make it easy).

WHICH DO YOU CHOOSE?

If you're overwhelmed by the idea of creating a website, I'd recommend starting with WordPress.com. Get the lowest paid plan so you can banish those pesky ads and have your own domain name. If in the future, if you decide to switch to self-hosted WordPress, you can.

If you aren't daunted by this, and want your site to work in the way you need it to without limitations, go for WordPress.org. If you like some of the WordPress.com features, you can add them with the free Jetpack plugin, going you the best of both worlds. If you know your site will grow over time, it's going to be easier if you start with the platform you plan to stick with.

AND IF YOU CHANGE YOUR MIND...

The good news is that switching between the two platforms is relatively easy. You can export all of your content from one to the other. And if you start out with WordPress.com, then I can all but guarantee that the theme and plugins you used will also be available on WordPress.org.

III

WORDPRESS.COM

4

CREATING A WORDPRESS.COM SITE

So, you've decided to go for a WordPress.com site. You want something easy and low-risk, and aren't worried about the relative lack of flexibility.

Great!

You'll be pleased to know that the process is very straightforward. Just follow these steps.

SIGNING UP FOR WORDPRESS

The first thing to do is get yourself a WordPress account. Go to WordPress.com (I bet you guessed that, didn't you, you clever thing?) and click the **Get Started** button.

Image 4-1 The WordPress.com signup screen

This will take you to the signup screen. You'll need to type in your email address, preferred username and password. There are limitations on how you can format passwords, for security.

Add the correct information and click the **Create your account** button.

WordPress will ask you what kind of site you're building. Don't worry too much about this: you can change it later, and all it does is activate some settings it thinks might be useful for you. Select **Professional**.

Now you'll be asked for your sector. Again, this isn't important. It won't affect anything about your site, but is used by Word-Press.com to monitor their usage across sectors. Type in whatever keyword you feel comfortable with (*Writing* or *Publishing* for example) and hit **Continue**.

Next, type in the name of your site. This will probably be your name (or your pen name). If you want to call it *Rachel's Fab Cat Memes Site*, that's up to you (but it might not enhance your career as a writer). This is another setting you can change at any time, so don't get too hung up on it.

Now you'll be asked for your site address. This is the bit that goes before *wordpress.com* in your domain name. So, if I want *rachelmccollin.wordpress.com*, I'd type *rachelmccollin* here.

Note: If you're planning on using your own domain name (and I'll show you how to do that in Chapter 8), this bit isn't too important. So go mad, if you want to. Motherofcats.wordpress.com, anyone?

WordPress will now give you the option to buy a domain name using the address you've typed in. There are clearly other Rachel McCollins using WordPress, so it's given me the very memorable *rachelmccollin644366076.wordpress.com* as my free option. Catchy!

For now, we're not going to buy a domain name, so keep experimenting, typing in an address at the top until it gives you a free domain that you like. If I type *rachelmcwrites*, it gives me *rachelmcwrites.wordpress.com*, which is much nicer.

Once you've got a domain you're happy with, click the **Select** button next to it.

Note: If you do want to buy your domain name at this stage, I recommend taking a look at Chapter 8 first. It'll give you some advice on choosing the right domain name for you.

Next, you'll need to pick a plan. Let's pause the signup process to take a look at the different plans and what they offer.

WORDPRESS.COM PLANS

At time of writing, these are the plans available (don't you just hate it when you have to choose between more than two?) and what they include, with a writerly emphasis.

FREE

The free plan is described as 'best for students' which makes me chuckle. As if students are the only people on a budget (I'm not saying students are wealthy, but nor are many writers).

It includes dozens of themes, which don't tend to have a lot of customization options, so you'll struggle to get yours looking professional (but it's not impossible).

It includes social media features like sharing buttons and the ability to auto-post new content to your social media accounts, and it lets you link directly to your MailChimp account.

So far so good, huh?

Well, yes and no. Don't forget that a free plan means ads will be added to your site. The site owners (not you, remember) get any money from this and you have no control over it.

You also won't be able to add your own domain.

But the good news is that you can upgrade at any time. So if you're just experimenting with WordPress.com right now, or you want to get started without spending any money, go ahead and pick the free plan.

BLOGGER

This is touted as being (guess what?) 'best for bloggers', but it only offers two benefits over the free plan: email support and a *.blog* domain. This means you can't use *authorname.com*, or whatever else you might have in mind. But you could use *authorname.blog*.

It costs three dollars a month at time of writing, but gives you no extra themes or features (apart from jettisoning those pesky ads). To be frank, you could get yourself a very basic hosting package for that money and have a self-hosted WordPress site with whatever features you want, although that probably wouldn't cover a domain name.

If you want a paid plan, I'd skip the Blogger option and look at the next one…

PERSONAL

The Personal plan has one benefit over the Blogger plan: you're not limited to a *.blog* domain name. You can pick whatever domain name you want, if it's available, and connect it to your site.

This will make your site look more professional, but you still don't get any extra features. So, let's take a look at Premium.

PREMIUM

This is the first package that offers significant benefits over the free plan.

You get more customization, advanced tools for things like SEO and performance, unlimited themes, and (of course) your own domain and no ads.

If you want one of the premium themes offered in this plan, but don't want to pay for the whole plan, you can just pay for the theme on top of your more basic plan. Find out how to do this at wp4writers.com/premiumthemes.

BUSINESS PLANS

If you really want to break the bank, there are business plans available too. These are very expensive and unlikely to be relevant to an author website. So take a look but I wouldn't recommend parting with your cash for these!

GETTING THINGS UP AND RUNNING

I'm going to imagine you're experimenting with WordPress for now, and going with a free plan.

Click on the **Start with Free** button. WordPress will take a few moments and get your site set up.

Now two things will happen:

- You'll be taken to the WordPress dashboard.
- You'll get an email asking you to confirm your email address.

While you're waiting for WordPress to work its magic, go on over to your email inbox to see if that email has arrived yet. When it does, click on the link to verify your email address. This will take you straight back to the WordPress dashboard (killing two birds with one stone).

YOUR NEW SITE

Now it's time to start exploring the WordPress dashboard.

When you first log in, you'll be taken to a setup screen, with the 'Welcome back!' message and a checklist showing what you've done and what you need to do.

Image 4-2 WordPress.com checklist

If you verified your email, it'll indicate that you've done that, as well as creating your site and updating your site title (in other words, adding the site title in the first place).

You'll have a list of things it tells you to do next, not all of which are mandatory.

Start by creating a tagline. This is a line of text that tells people a bit more about you. In most themes, it'll sit either next to or below your site title at the top of every page. For example, on my fiction site, my tagline is 'Thrillers that make you think'.

Click the **Do it!** button to set up your tagline and save it. If you can't think of a tagline right now, don't worry: you can come back and add one (or change it) at any time.

Work your way through the checklist, filling out the bits you're ready to. The wizard will tell you what to do at each stage, so you don't need me to tell you too.

If you don't want to fill out all the elements on the to-do list (and let's face it, you're probably itching to get started on actually, you know, creating a working site), just move your mouse over to the menu on the left-hand side and select any one of the options. The **View Site** option is a good one to start with, as it'll show you what your site looks like right now.

Image 4-3 Site in progress

Now, if your site is anything like mine right now, you might be grasping at your hair and trying to tear it out. Or you might be staring at the screen with your mouth wide and your brow creased into a frown so deep my cat could hide in it.

Looks terrible, doesn't it?

Don't worry. Mine looks awful too, and I'm going to help you make it look great in the next few chapters.

But before we do that, let's take a look at what's on offer in the WordPress dashboard.

(If you want to roll your sleeves up and start tinkering with your site, by all means do so: you can come back to this chapter at any time as a handy reference.)

THE WORDPRESS DASHBOARD

The WordPress dashboard includes a bunch of screens that will help you manage your site and add content to it. You access all of these via the admin menu on the left-hand side.

Let's take a look at some of those menu items.

Note: The WordPress.com dashboard and the WordPress.org dashboard are different. To find out about the WordPress.org dashboard, go to Chapter 11.

VIEW SITE

This is the screen that lets you preview your site. Of course, you can always do that by having another browser window open alongside the admin screens, and opening your site in that. But this way is quicker.

Use it to test changes and check that everything looks as you expect it to on the front end.

So far, it's probably your least favorite menu item, as you used it to see just how horrible your site is looking right now. But once you've got your site configured and some content added, the **View Site** link will be your friend.

STATS

This is a nifty feature of WordPress.com that tells you how many people have been viewing your site. You can view your stats by day, week, month or year and you can see how many views your site has had as well as how many unique visitors.

What's the difference between views and unique visitors?

A view is logged every time someone views your site. It doesn't matter who's viewing it: every time they visit it will be one view. So if I visit your site ten times, that's ten views.

A unique visitor is a unique individual (or more precisely, a unique computer, tablet or mobile phone) visiting your site. So if I visit your site ten times, that's logged as one unique visit.

Don't worry too much about your website stats. I know authors are tempted to check out their stats every three and a half seconds; I know I sometimes refresh my sales figures that often. But you'll only need to look at the stats if there's a problem with your site or if you want to analyze which posts get the most traffic. This can help you identify what topics to write more about. I'll cover this in more detail in Chapter 17.

ACTIVITY

This is one of those strange little features of WordPress that I can't see much point of. It tracks all of the things you recently did on your site.

If you want to be reminded that you just published a post or changed your site description, then by all means check out your activity.

If you've got more interesting things to do with your time, just ignore it.

PLAN

Here's where you go to upgrade to a premium plan if you decide you need one in the future. If you're happy with your plan, it's just another option to ignore.

MANAGE

Now we're getting into the fun stuff (can you tell I don't get out much?). This is the section of the admin menu where you can start creating content.

The content types available to you are:

- **Site Pages**. Static pages like your 'About Me' page and your contact page.
- **Blog Posts**. The posts you add on a regular basis to keep your readers updated.
- **Media**. Images, files and other media. You can add those via this link or simply insert them into posts when you're creating those. I tend to add them to posts when I need them. More on media in Chapter 23.
- **Comments**. Use this option to read the comments people have left on your posts and to reply to them (or spam them if needs be). Commenting is a great way to build up a rapport between you and your fans.

- **Feedback**. Here's where you'll find any entries that have been made in your site's contact forms. I have no idea why they call it feedback: a visitor might fill out a form to give you feedback, or they might fill it out to just say hi.
- **Plugins**. Here you can install extra plugins to give your site more features. How many are available to you will depend on your plan. If you're on the free plan, you won't be able to install plugins; the lowest plan that lets you install plugins is the Business plan (boo!). If you want to add plugins to your site, ignore WordPress.com and go with WordPress.org instead: your wallet will thank you for it.
- **Import**. If you had another website before this one and you want to import all of your posts and pages, this feature will let you do it without having to manually copy and paste things across. It's compatible with other WordPress sites (of course), as well as Medium, Blogger, Wix, Squarespace and some more obscure blogging platforms that if you're anything like me, you've never heard of. You can find out how to do this in Chapter 19.

If you want to know more about content (and are too impatient to read through to that bit, tsk), check out Chapters 12 and 18.

PERSONALIZE

This section has just one item: **Customize**. This is where you get to choose the theme for your site and configure how it'll look.

We'll come back to the **Customize** option in more detail in Chapter 13.

CONFIGURE

The Configure section has some options that let you configure the way your site works. Most of these are things you'll only look at once, or maybe not at all.

- **Earn**. Only available with the Premium plan (is this starting to sound familiar?), this option lets you make money from your website by enabling ads that you get paid for. This is different from the ads displayed on a free site, as you have no control over those and don't get any money from them (but you do get a free website, so you can't complain too much).
- **Sharing**. This is one of my favorite features of WordPress.com. It lets you automatically share all your new blog posts to your social media accounts, without lifting a finger. Simply link your site to Facebook, Twitter, LinkedIn and/or Tumblr, and leave it to work on its own. We'll look at this again in Chapter 24.
- **People**. Here you can add more people to your site, as long as they have a WordPress.com account. So if you have someone who manages your blog posts, checks your stats, configures your theme, or anything else, you can add them here and they'll have access to the site. There are different levels of access, depending on what you want them to be able to do: **Viewer** (can follow the site and visit it but not edit it or access the dashboard), **Contributor** (can write posts but not publish them), **Author** (can write and publish their own posts), **Editor** (can write posts and publish their own and others' posts), and **Administrator** (can do everything an editor can do and access site settings too).
- **Domains**. If you want to set up your own domain name, here's where you do it.
- **Settings**. Everything not covered in the other screens! Here you can do things like update your site title and tagline, change the way your site content is displayed, manage the way comments work and set up a nifty 'related posts' feature.

You can either take some time to check out all of these options now and familiarize yourself with the system, or you can come back to them when you need them.

SHORTCUTS

Sometimes you're feeling lazy. You don't want to be bothered with the effort of clicking on the admin menu with the mouse and accessing a menu item. Life's too short, darling.

WordPress.com has your back. There's a shortcut you can use to do the most frequent task quickly. And what is that task? Writing a new blog post, of course.

To start creating a new post from wherever you are in Word-Press.com, just click the **Write** link at the top right of your screen. It'll open up a new screen for you, a blank canvas ready for your words of wisdom.

I'll show you just how to use that screen and publish your posts in the next chapter.

AND THERE'S A COMMUNITY...

Here's another fab feature of WordPress.com. It's a community of bloggers. You can follow other blogs, comment on each other's posts, and invite people to follow you.

To invite people to follow you, go to the **People** option in the **Configure** section of the admin menu. There, you can invite people to join your site as viewers.

To view the latest posts on the blogs you follow, click on the **Reader** link right at the top of your screen, next to the **My Site** link.

Here you can keep up to date with the sites you follow as well as discovering new sites that interest you. This is a great way to interact with other writers. Anyone with a WordPress.com site will be part of this community, as well as anyone running a WordPress.org site with the Jetpack plugin enabled.

So that's an overview of the WordPress.com dashboard. Now let's move on to creating some content—your first post and page.

5

CREATING YOUR FIRST CONTENT

BEFORE YOU START CUSTOMIZING your site and making it look good, it's sensible to add just a few posts and pages, so that you have some content you can see when you're trying out design options.

I'll cover creating posts and pages in more detail in Chapters 21-22, but for now, let's just quickly get a couple of each published.

CREATING A POST

There are two ways to create a post: either click the **Write** link at the top right of the screen, or go to **Blog Posts > Add** in the admin menu on the left-hand side.

You'll now see the blank screen for creating your post.

Start by typing in the post title. Then either hit **Return** on your keyboard or click into the box for your first paragraph. Just type as you normally would. Every time you hit **Return**, a new block will be created. Each block represents a paragraph of text. You can convert your paragraphs to lists, headings, or other text blocks, or you can create blocks for images or other media.

Blocks and post creation are covered in much more detail in Chapter 20; for now, we're just creating a dummy post. Type whatever you fancy into the post (remember you can always delete this later, so have fun).

Once you're happy with your post (remember, this is a dummy post; you'll spend longer crafting your exquisite tracts of literary loveliness later), click on the **Publish** button, which you'll find at the top right of the screen.

You'll be presented with a few pre-publish checks. These are really useful when you come to write 'proper' posts for your blog, as they help you check the post is ready before you publish it. But for now, don't fret. Just hit the **Publish** button again.

Now, repeat that to create your second post. To add another post, click the back arrow at the top left of the screen, and go to **Blog Posts > Add** or click that **Write** button in the top menu bar.

Add some content to your post (don't worry about what it is yet), and publish it.

Lovely!

CREATING A PAGE

Your site is also going to need a few pages. We're not going to create them all here, but you will need two to help you with setting up your menu and your home page settings.

To get started, create two pages: one called 'Home' and one called 'Blog'.

To create a page, go to **Site Pages > Add**. Give your page a title of *Home*. For the home page, type in some content (don't worry about what this is just yet, you can come back to it later). Click the **Publish** button to publish it, then click **Publish** again.

Now do the same for the Blog page. To add another page, click the back arrow on the top left of the screen and click **Site Pages > Add** again.

This time, leave the page empty. WordPress will automatically populate this page with your blog posts: you don't need to add anything.

Publish your empty post, and go back to the main menu by clicking the back arrow at the top left of the screen.

You now have two pages in your site.

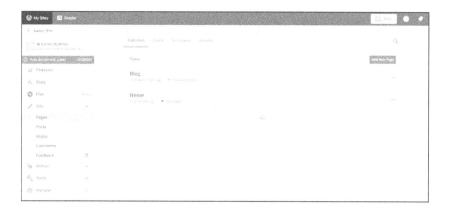

Image 5-1 Published pages in the WordPress.com dashboard

Over time, you'll want to add more content to your site, of course. The process for doing this is the same for WordPress.com and for self-hosted WordPress. So skip on over to Chapter 18 if you want to know more. Or alternatively, stick around here with the WordPress.com folks and learn how to get your site looking good.

TIME TO GET TWEAKING!

Tweaking the site and theme settings is much easier if you have some content on your site, as you can see what effect your changes will have on your content.

Now we've quickly created those two posts and two pages, let's move on to customizing the theme settings.

6

GETTING YOUR SITE LOOKING PRETTY: THEMES

So, you've got a shiny new website, but…

Hang on a minute.

It isn't shiny at all. In fact, you've clicked the **View Site** link to check it out and it looks godawful.

Never fear. Here's where you'll make it better.

WHAT THEMES CAN YOU USE? IT DEPENDS…

The first thing to do is choose a theme. How many themes you have available to you will depend on your plan, and will change over time as new themes are developed.

To pick your theme, go to **Personalize > Customize > Theme**. In other words, clink on the **Theme** button in the admin menu, next to **Customize** (why it isn't a separate menu item, I can't tell you).

You'll be confronted with a grid of themes you can choose from. Even with a free plan, there are plenty to start with. In fact, you might find yourself overwhelmed by the themes on offer, especially if you've opted for a premium plan.

So you'll need some criteria to help you choose your theme.

CHOOSING THE THEME FOR YOUR SITE

You want your site to reflect your brand as an author.

Now, if you're throwing the book at the wall and telling me to stop sounding all corporate, I apologize.

But branding is important for authors. Your brand consists of everything public about you as a writer, and it helps people understand what kind of writer you are.

This will include visual elements such as your book covers, and less tangible elements such as the way you interact on social media and the tone of your writing. If you've spent time developing your craft (and if you haven't, put this book down RIGHT NOW. You need to do that before you send any time faffing around with a website), you'll have your own unique authorial voice.

Sounds posh, doesn't it? I know. I didn't even realize I had a voice until one of my stories was read out anonymously at an event and the person next to me said, "that's yours, isn't it?" Turns out he'd recognized my writing style. I can tell you I did a little happy dance that day.

So, to get back to the matter at hand.

There are two aspects of your website that will reflect your brand:

- Your content: the topics you cover and the way you write.
- The visual design: the way everything looks.

Choosing a theme will be how you determine the visual design of your site. So take some time to analyze your brand:

- What colors do you have on your book covers?
- What fonts?
- Any effects like grungy background or sparkles?
- Is the overall tone light or dark, serious or humorous?

If you work with a cover designer (and I recommend it, even if you're self-published), ask them what colors and fonts they use. You may be able to replicate the fonts in your site and you'll certainly be able to use colors which are either very similar or exactly the same.

So, when you're choosing your theme, look for:

- Color.
- Mood.
- Font styles.
- White space (or not).

All of these are things you can type into the search box to help you find the right theme. So if you're a contemporary romance writer with lighthearted, fun covers in shades of blue and pink, you might type *fun blue pink* into the search bar.

Another approach is to use a theme with lots of customization options. These themes let you manually change the colors and/or fonts. This gives you the highest level of control. So search for *customize* when you're looking for your theme.

I think there are some WordPress.com themes that are more suited to author websites than others. But since the list changes regularly, instead of listing them here, I've added a list to my blog. You can find it at wp4writers.com/comthemes.

It may take you some time to find the right theme for you. This is important, so don't skimp. In fact, this will be about half of the total work in setting up your site. If you choose a theme that you later realize isn't right for you, don't worry: you can switch your theme at any time. You won't lose any of your posts or pages, but you will have to set your menu and widgets up again (more of which later in this chapter).

TWEAKING YOUR THEME

Now it's time to get your theme looking as good as it possibly can.

The precise way you do this will vary depending on your theme, as different themes have different settings. But the principles are similar.

Once you've found your theme, you'll need to tweak it with the Customizer, which you access by clicking **Customize** in the admin menu.

I'm going to be using the Shoreditch theme, because it has a rather nifty feature that lets you add panels to the home page. I'm going to use one of those as a link to my landing page.

I won't go into how you do this in detail here, but if you want to see how to use the free Shoreditch theme (which you can also get for free with a self-hosted WordPress site), go to wp4writers.com/shoreditch.

CUSTOMIZING COLORS

If your theme allows it, click on the **Colors & Backgrounds** (or **Colors**) option to tweak the color settings.

You won't be able to change many of the colors manually, but many themes include a range of color palettes to choose from. You might also be able to manually set the main color in the theme, which could be the background color, or the color of your headings: it'll all depend on the theme.

I've chosen a color scheme for my site which will coordinate with an image I plan to add to my home page. Don't forget this is something you can always change later—nothing is set in stone.

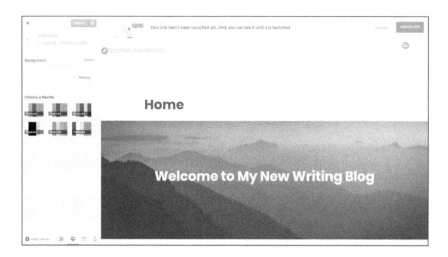

Image 6-1 Customizing colors

Once you're happy with your choice, click the **Publish** button at the top of the Customizer menu. If you don't do this, your changes won't be saved.

CUSTOMIZING FONTS

If your theme lets you customize the fonts, it'll be easier to make your site fit with your brand.

Click on the **Fonts** option in the Customizer screen and select the font for your headings and body text. You'll be given a list of fonts to choose from: experiment until you find one that is as close as possible to those used on your book covers.

Image 6-2 Customizing fonts

No free WordPress.com theme will let you select from every available font or any color scheme: but if these are features you need, search for them when you're looking for a theme and be prepared to pay for the privilege. Alternatively, self-hosted Word-Press has plenty of free themes with more customization options.

Again, once you're happy with your choices, click the **Publish** button to save.

CUSTOMIZING THE HOME PAGE

Now let's work on the home page.

In the Customizer, click the **Homepage settings** option. This will open up an area on the left where you can change your settings.

Our site has a static home page and the 'Blog' page for blog posts. So we need to change the settings to reflect this.

Click the **A static page** option. You'll then be given two drop-down lists: one for the Homepage and one for the Posts page. Select **Home** and then **Blog**, respectively.

Once again, click **Publish** to save your changes.

Help! What if I want my blog posts on my home page?

Good question. Most authors choose to have a static page as their home page so they can introduce themselves and tell the visitor about how the site works.

But if you're a nonfiction author your blog will be more important, so you may choose to display blog posts on the home page.

You can always come back and change this later if you want. If you do decide to use your home page for blog posts, you can delete that 'Blog' page as WordPress will automatically generate your home page for you.

Here are some other things you can customize:

- Header image (if your theme includes one). Upload your banner image here if you have one. Many themes will restrict the dimensions of this banner, and no free themes will let you turn it into a clickable link. If you want a flexible banner with no restrictions on the dimensions of the image, type in *flexible header image* as a search term when searching for a theme. For details of some premium themes (and WordPress.org themes) that let you create a clickable banner in the header, go to wp4writers.com/clickableheaders.
- Other theme options. Some themes have a **Theme Options** item in the Customizer. If your theme comes with one of these, click on it and see what it gives you. Some of the options can only be unlocked by upgrading to premium, but you may strike lucky and have some freebies.
- Menus and Widgets. Be patient! Those come next.

You may have more customization options, depending on your theme.

Spend some time experimenting. You can always come back and make changes if you need to. And remember your site isn't live yet so you can do whatever you want without anyone else being able to see it.

HELPING VISITORS FIND THEIR WAY AROUND WITH A MENU

A navigation menu will help visitors find their way around your site. It's normal to include just static pages in your menu, such as the home page, contact page, 'About me' page and blog.

Depending on your theme, your navigation menu will be at the top of the page, in the top right hand corner, or below the header. Which you prefer will be one of the factors in choosing your theme.

To create a menu, go to **Customize > Menus**. WordPress will have created a menu called **Primary** for you, which will be empty. Click on that.

To add items, click the **Add items** button, then select **Pages**. Select the pages you want to add to your menu, which right now will be **Home** and **Blog**.

Why have the home page in my menu, when people can get to it by clicking on my name in the header?

It can be tempting to slim down your menu by removing the link to the home page.

But it's good practice to have it here as well as via your site title. (If you weren't aware of the link in the site title, try clicking it and see what happens.)

This is because some people will only expect one or the other, and others will be using assistive technology that makes it difficult for them to access the link in the site title.

So make sure you have a link to the home page in the menu, and make it the first menu item.

Once you're happy with your menu, click **Publish** to save it.

ADDING WIDGETS FOR EXTRA TIDBITS

Another nifty feature of WordPress is widgets. These are snippets of content that sit in the sidebar or footer of your site.

The spots you have available to you for widgets will depend on your theme. Some themes just have one sidebar widget area. Others let you add widgets to the home page. And others have widget areas in the footer, at the bottom of the page.

Widgets, sidebars, widget areas: what's the difference?

The terminology around WordPress widgets can be confusing to say the least. So let's try to clear up some of the jargon.

A **widget** is a snippet of content or code that you can add to every page in your site. Examples are lists of posts, social media feeds and newsletter signup forms. These aren't part of any post, but sit outside it in a widget area.

A **widget area** is an area on the pages in your site where you can place widgets. The widget areas are defined in your theme, and may be in a sidebar (next to the content) or the footer (below the content)—or both. Some themes even have widget areas in the header or on the home page.

A **sidebar** is an area of space in your page which is to the side of the main content. Sometimes you'll hear sidebars and widget areas referred to interchangeably, but they aren't the same thing. Your sidebar is probably just one of the widget areas in your site.

I'm going to assume that your theme has at least one widget area, and that'll be in the sidebar. It might be called 'Sidebar', 'Sidebar Number 1', or anything else the theme developer chose to call it (helpful, huh?), but it'll include the word 'sidebar' in there somewhere.

In the Customizer, click on **Widgets**, and then on **Sidebar** (or whatever yours is called). WordPress has probably added one or two widgets in there already: in my site, it's added a Follow widget and a Search widget. Both useful, so I'm going to leave them there.

To add another widget, click on (you guessed it) **Add a Widget**.

You'll now be presented with a list of the widgets available to you. There are lots of them: take some time to scroll down and have a look at them.

For now, let's add the **Recent Posts** widget. Click on that and it'll be added to the widget area (you'll see it listed on the left).

Now you can type in whatever title you want to give it (I'm calling mine *What I'm writing about*), and the number of posts you want to display (let's go for six).

WordPress will have a little think, the wheels will spin, and then your widget will appear in the sidebar, with those two posts you already created.

Now you see why I got you to take time out and create those first? I know what I'm doing (honest).

Image 6-3 Widgets in WordPress.com

If you want to change the order of the widgets in your widget area, just drag them into the correct order. Once you're happy, don't forget to click **Publish** to save your changes.

And if your site has widget areas elsewhere, such as in the footer, take some time to add widgets there. Or you can come back and do it later, it's up to you. You might want to come back to this after Chapter 24, when you've learned about linking your site to your social media accounts—then you can add a Facebook widget, for example.

LAUNCHING YOUR SITE

Before anyone will be able to see your site, you'll need to launch it. You can do this now if you want. Or you can wait until everything is perfect—it depends on how ready you feel.

If you do decide to launch your site now, make sure you tidy it up first. Make sure those dummy posts and pages look good and aren't full of junk. If you want, delete them and replace them with some proper ones, or leave the site with no posts just yet. It'll look a bit forlorn, but that's better than having your trashy dummy posts littering your site.

To launch your site, click the **Launch** button at the top right of the screen. WordPress will (unhelpfully) take you back to a sales screen, where it's trying to convince you to upgrade before launching. Ignore all this and stick to your guns.

Work through the launch process and you'll get an email telling you your site is live. You'll also start getting a series of emails about your site. Some of these are useful, and give you tips on managing your site. But some are designed to persuade you to upgrade, and are frankly annoying in my opinion. Feel free to delete them!

7

ADDING EXTRA WHIZZINESS: BONUS FEATURES

IF YOU WANT to make your WordPress.com site stand out from the crowd, there are a few extra features you can use to make your website shine.

These features are a bit random, which is why they didn't fit nicely in any of the previous chapters. So here they are, in their own 'random bits of awesomeness' chapter.

PORTFOLIOS

WordPress.com lets you add two types of custom post type: portfolios and testimonials.

Custom post types? What's one of those?

WordPress comes with a bunch of post types that you can use without having to activate any extra features. These are posts, pages and attachments (i.e. media). With WordPress.org, you can add as many extra post types as you want, and these are called custom post types. For example, you would create a 'product' post type if you're adding a store to your site.

With WordPress.com you can't add your own post types, but you can activate testimonials and/or portfolios if you want.

For an author website, the best use of portfolios is for books. By activating the portfolios post type, you can add a 'project' post for each of your books and then add a list of all of them (with a link to the page for the individual book) to any page in your site.

To activate portfolios, go to **Manage > Settings** and select the **Writing** tab. Scroll down to the **Content types** section and toggle **Portfolio Projects** to on.

You'll then find that **Portfolio** appears in the **Site** section of the admin menu. Click here to add new projects, one for each of your books. You can also add a project type to each project, which might be useful for creating series.

To add a list of your books to a page, create the new page and then within the content, type in the shortcode *[portfolio]* (making sure you use the square brackets). You can add parameters to this to customize the way your portfolio will appear—see wp4writers.com/portfolios for more details. There are some powerful options for displaying your projects in columns and including/excluding project types—so you could use the shortcode with the appropriate parameters for each of your series.

Your books will all be listed on the page after you publish it. A neat way to add information about all of your books to one summary page as well as in individual pages.

RELATED POSTS

The Related Posts feature is designed to encourage people to stick around on your site and read more. It displays a list of similar posts at the bottom of each post, using post metadata such as the category and tags as well as the content itself to decide which posts are related.

To activate it, go to **Tools > Marketing** and go to the **Related Posts** section. Toggle **Show related content after posts** to on.

You can also opt to show a 'Related' heading which makes it clearer what this is, and to display the featured image for each related post. If you're using featured images (something I recommend and you can learn more about in Chapter 23), then this will make it easier for people to click on those posts, and make them more enticing.

SLIDESHOWS AND IMAGE CAROUSELS

WordPress.com also lets you add a bit of oomph to the images in your posts by displaying them as slideshows or image carousels.

To activate these, go to **Manage > Settings** and select the **Writing** tab. Scroll down to the **Media** section.

Try them out and see how it makes the images in your site look. If your site is very image-heavy, it could make it look a whole lot better. Or you might find that your theme already does a great job with images.

8

ME.COM: USING YOUR OWN DOMAIN

So FAR, we've been working with a free WordPress.com account. This gives you basic features like a blog and social sharing, and helps you to get online.

But if you want a professional author website you'll need your own domain name. In this chapter, I'll show you how to set one up with WordPress.com.

WHY REGISTER YOUR OWN DOMAIN?

Good question. You might be thinking that you've got yourself a perfectly good website at *worldsbestauthor.wordpress.com*. (I have no idea if that is a real domain and if you're tempted by it: don't. Please. Step away right now.)

But wouldn't it be so much better if you could have *worldsbestauthor.com*? (Again, please don't. People will hate you.)

OK, let's be serious. Chances are you're going to use your own name for this. So I'm sure you agree that *rachelmccollin.com* is so much easier for me to tell people when I meet them, and looks so much more professional in the back matter of my books, that *rachelmccollin.wordpress.com*?

If you want to be a professional author (and I'm assuming you do, because you picked up this book, you clever thing), then you want to project a professional image. Having your own domain name is part of that.

WHERE TO START: THE OPTIONS FOR CHOOSING AND REGISTERING A DOMAIN

So, you've decided to get your own domain name. Good for you!

The first step is to identify if it's already taken. You can check this in the WordPress dashboard or you can simply type it into a browser. Try it.

You'll get one of three results:

- A screen telling you this domain doesn't exist. Hurrah!
- Someone else's website. Sorry, it's already taken.
- A screen informing you that someone else has registered the domain name and is happy to sell it to you for an exorbitant fee.

If you do discover that someone else is sitting on your ideal domain name, don't worry too much. You have my permission to scream at the wall a little bit. You also have my permission to post an angry tweet about domain squatters and the fact that they're parasites on the internet (sorry, rant over). You then have my permission to delete that tweet. Seriously, take it down right away—your readers don't care.

But don't—please, please don't—get into negotiations to buy the domain name. It's just not worth it.

There's a nice story about a group of guys who came up with a great scam when they were sitting in the pub, sometime in the 1990s. It occurred to them that 20th Century Fox would want to change its name to 21st Century Fox once the 21st century rolled around. They did a bit of research and found that no one had registered the trademark yet. So they decided to register it themselves, in the expectation that they'd make a killing from Fox when they spotted it.

What happened? Well, ask yourself this: have you seen '21st Century Fox' in the opening screen to any movie?

(If you don't believe me, go see *Spiderman: Homecoming*. It may be Marvel but it was made by Fox. And it's a great movie.)

If your perfect domain name is not available, don't be tempted to pay over a pile of cash to get it. It just isn't worth it. Most people don't type domain names into their browser anyway (in fact, I'm not sure anyone under the age of twenty knows what that means); they'll search for you instead.

So if you have a domain name that's relevant to you, is easy to reel off at all those cocktail parties you go to, and is available, go with that.

The good news is that WordPress.com not only lets you register the domain, it also lets you find the right one.

Let's take a look at how it works.

REGISTERING A DOMAIN NAME VIA WORDPRESS.COM

WordPress.com makes it super easy to register a domain name and associate it with your site.

Go to **Plan > Domains**. You'll see a screen with your current domain name.

Click the **Add Domain** button. WordPress will make some suggestions based on your existing domain name (i.e. the bit before the *.wordpress.com*).

Type in your name or the title you'd like to use for your site, all as one word. So I'm going to type in *rachelmccollin*.

WordPress will then pause for a moment while it fetches available domain names, and give you some suggestions. I've very sensibly been given *rachelmccollin.net*, and rather less sensibly, *mccoll.democrat*. I'm not even American! I haven't been offered *rachelmc-*

collin.com as I already have that registered for another site running on WordPress.org.

Scroll down until you find one you like. Click the **Upgrade** button next to it.

You'll be given the option to pay a bit more for the ability to use your email address using Gmail. If you want to use your domain name for email as well as your website (something I recommend), this is by far the easiest way to do it. If you aren't sure, you can always come back and add it later if you want.

What is GSuite?

GSuite is a service from Google that lets you associate your own domain name with a Gmail account. So instead of using *rachelmccollin@gmail.com* (which probably isn't available anyway), I can use *myemail@rachelmccollin.com*, or anything else I like *@rachelmccollin.com*.

It's a great way to get yourself a professional email address and get access to it using the world's most popular email system. You can find out more about it at wp4writers.com/gmail.

If you want to set up email, type in the email address you want to use and click the **Yes, Add Email** button. If you don't (or you want to come back to this later), just click the (rather less obvious) **Skip** button.

You'll then be presented with a screen where you input some information on you as a domain registrant and decide whether to opt for privacy. Once you've done this, you'll be taken to the checkout.

Your domain name will now work perfectly with your Word-Press.com site. If someone types in your new domain name in their browser, they'll be taken to your WordPress.com site. And they need never know that your site is built on WordPress.com

Registering a domain name means you've upgraded from a free plan. This will also remove those pesky ads from your site. Bonus!

CONNECTING A DOMAIN NAME REGISTERED ELSEWHERE

If you've already registered your domain name, because you were one of those clever people who foresaw the importance of the internet back in 1996 and registered every variation of your name (or maybe because you just fancied owning your own domain name), then you can configure that to work in just the same way as a domain you register via WordPress.com.

Go to **Plan > Domains**. Click the **Add Domain** button.

Scroll down to the **Already own a domain?** option and click on **Use a domain I own**.

You're now given two options: you can either transfer your domain into WordPress.com, or point it to WordPress.com from your current registrar.

Transferring it to WordPress.com is the simplest option, but might not always be the best. You should stick with your existing registrar if any of the following apply:

- You plan to move away from WordPress.com in the future, or think you might (perhaps switching to WordPress.org).
- You're already using your domain name for an email address.

Keeping your domain name with your existing registrar gives you more control, although you can transfer it out of Word-Press.com again in the future if you need to. But if you'd rather switch it to WordPress.com, then select that option.

Whichever option you choose, WordPress will give you instructions on how to proceed. The details of this will vary depending on your existing registrar: just follow what WordPress tells you and you can't go far wrong. And if you have problems during the process, you can always get help from the WordPress support team at support.wordpress.com.

CONGRATULATIONS! YOU NOW HAVE A WORDPRESS.COM SITE

Huh? It doesn't look like much.

Don't worry. You're not done yet. But your site is up and running and you have the bones of an author website.

The next part of this book deals with setting up a site on Word-Press.com, so you can skip that. Instead, head for Chapter 17 where you can start learning how to create content.

IV

SELF-HOSTED WORDPRESS

9

GETTING STARTED: HOSTING AND DOMAINS

So you've decided to future-proof your author career and get yourself a website that's entirely yours?

One with almost limitless flexibility, a vast community of users and developers, and an interface that's being constantly developed to make it more user-friendly?

Congratulations. I'm a huge fan of self-hosted WordPress and believe it's the best website system out there for anyone who's serious about having a professional online presence.

I'm not alone: hundreds of best-selling authors, both independent and traditionally published, use WordPress to host their website.

Anyway, I'll stop the sales pitch now. You're here, already. And you want to know how to get started.

The first thing to do is to find yourself a hosting provider. Once you've done that, you'll need a domain name. The good news is you can do both of those at the same time.

So let's get started.

FINDING A HOSTING PROVIDER

This is the aspect of WordPress.org that's the most different from WordPress.com. With WordPress.com, the platform is your hosting provider. But with WordPress.org, you can install the software wherever you want. If you were feeling brave you could get a server running in your bedroom, hook it up to the internet, and take it from there. But I really don't recommend that.

Instead, you'll need to rent server space from a hosting provider. There are lots of these out there, and it can be daunting to choose one. So here are some criteria to help you decide:

- Do they offer twenty-four-hour support?
- Do they offer an uptime guarantee, so you get money back if your site goes down through no fault of your own?
- Do they have good reviews and ratings from independent sources (try googling the name of the provider followed by 'reviews')?
- Do they include cPanel with your hosting plan? This is a dashboard that lets you manage your hosting and domain name. You'll rarely need to touch it but if you don't have it, you have less control.
- Do they offer a one-click WordPress installer? This makes installing WordPress quick and easy, although you may prefer to install the software manually (which isn't as hard as you think).
- Do they offer a WordPress-specific hosting plan? Providers who know WordPress will be better placed to answer all of your questions.
- Do they have an email address or phone number you can use to contact them if you need to? Some companies hide behind their support desk (not literally: you won't find them crouching in a corner behind the office furniture), and if you're not getting the help you need there, you need an alternative.

- If you contact them to ask questions about their services, do they reply? Does their reply make sense or is it full of jargon?
- Are they on this list: wp4writers.com/hosting? This is a list of recommended providers which I keep updated on my website. I'm not going to that list to this book as I don't want to give you information that might be out of date if you're reading this months after I wrote it. Just follow the link if you want my recommendations.

That's a lot of questions, but finding the right hosting provider is important as it will save you a lot of headaches in the long run.

Once you've found a provider, you'll need to choose a hosting plan.

CHOOSING A HOSTING PLAN

Every hosting provider has multiple hosting plans, and picking one can be daunting.

It's made a bit simpler if you understand that there are three main differentiators:

- The space allocated to you and the features bundled with your plan.
- Whether you have a private server or a virtual private server(known as VPS).
- Whether your hosting is based in the cloud or in a physical location.

Let's take the easiest one first.

PRICE AND FEATURES

The cheaper the plan, the less space you have, and the fewer features. For an author website, you can get away with most providers' cheapest plan, as you aren't going to need a lot of server space.

When it comes to features, choose the cheapest plan that includes cPanel. You might also want to pick a plan that includes a domain name, as this can be cheaper than registering a domain name separately.

VIRTUAL PRIVATE SERVERS

For an author website, you don't need to worry about this. VPS is for large, high-traffic sites that need to be exceptionally robust.

When you're starting out, this won't be you. And if your career ever reaches the point where your site is getting hammered and you need VPS, then you'll be raking it in and you can hire someone to worry about all of this for you. I don't imagine JK Rowling is personally responsible for ensuring the Pottermore website is on the best hosting plan!

In short—ignore plans with VPS. They'll be too expensive anyway.

CLOUD-BASED HOSTING

Cloud-based hosting is a relatively new concept, which is designed to give you a better guarantee of uptime.

Because your site is hosted in the cloud and not just on one server, it means that if one server has problems, another server can start delivering your site to visitors.

Unless you're based in a part of the world where it's difficult to get local hosting, or you can find a cloud-based hosting plan that's cheaper than a standard one, ignore cloud-based hosting.

TL;DR—PICKING A PLAN

Pick the cheapest plan that says it's suitable for WordPress and includes cPanel. That should meet your needs.

REGISTERING A DOMAIN

Once you have your hosting, you'll also need to register a domain.

I strongly recommend doing this at the same time as you buy hosting. Most hosting providers will throw in a domain name with all but their very cheapest hosting plans, and it means the hosting and domain will work together from the beginning.

Your hosting provider will give you the option to register a new domain while you're going through the process of signing up for hosting. Try the domain name that's ideal for you—*authorname.com*, for example. If that isn't available, don't worry. You'll have the option to choose another one: *authorname.net*, for example, or *authornamewrites.com*. If you write nonfiction, you might prefer to use a domain name related to your subject matter instead of your own name. But beware being too specific—if you broaden your writing topics in the future and start writing about the wildlife of the Norfolk Broads as well as the windmills of the Dutch lowlands, the domain name *dutch-windmills.com* won't be much use.

Work through the process of setting up your hosting and registering the domain name at the same time, and you'll be ready to start creating your site.

What if I already have a domain?

Good question.

If you've already registered your domain name and you want to use it with your new site, you can do one of two things: transfer your domain name to your new hosting provider (which shouldn't cost anything), or point your domain name to your new hosting.

Either way, when you sign up for hosting, you should be given an option to select this. Work through the steps provided and if you get stuck, remember that the support teams at hosting providers are always very keen to help anyone who's in the process of signing up—they want to win your business.

If in doubt, google the name of your hosting provider, followed by 'point domain name to account'.

You'll now have a hosting account and a domain name pointing to it. But you don't have a website yet. How do you install Word-Press and get your site set up?

Worry not, fair reader. I've got you covered. Just keep reading.

10

INSTALLING WORDPRESS: EASIER THAN YOU THINK

FOR MANY PEOPLE, this is either number one or number two on the list of reasons not to use self-hosted WordPress.

The two things that can put people off are getting hosting and installing the software.

But you've already got yourself some hosting, so that's one hurdle jumped. The second hurdle is easier to cross than you might think.

THE OPTIONS FOR INSTALLING WORDPRESS

There are two ways of installing WordPress: manually, or with the click of a button.

For most non-techies, the click of a button option is easily the preferred option. But just in case you are a techie, I'm going to help you to do it manually too.

Each method has its own advantages and disadvantages.

AUTOMATIC INSTALLATION

Pros:

- It's easy.
- It works.

Cons:

- Your hosting provider might add some extra code or plugins, which could cause you problems in the long run. Or might just annoy you. For most people, this isn't an issue.
- A poor hosting provider might not install the latest version of WordPress. A good one will.
- If your hosting provider doesn't provide cPanel as part of your package, you might not have access to an auto-installer (which is why this is an important criterion when choosing hosting). Some providers don't give you cPanel but do give you an auto-installer in their own dashboard.

MANUAL INSTALLATION

Pros:

- You get a clean installation with no extra code or plugins

Cons:

- It takes longer.
- It's not as easy.
- Sometimes it doesn't work properly (although that's normally due to user error).

For 90% of website owners, the automatic installation is absolutely fine. It's only if you're planning to customize the code in your site that you may have issues. But I'm assuming that you picked up this book because you have no intention of writing code.

If you fancy trying your hand at manual installation, read through the instructions below and give it a go if you want. But if you prefer an easy life, go with the automatic option.

INSTALLING WORDPRESS WITH AN AUTO-INSTALLER

So let's start with the quick and easy option.

First, you'll need to access your control panel with your hosting provider. This is normally called cPanel, although some providers give it a snazzy (and confusing) name of their own.

If you're not sure how to get to this, check the email you received when you set up your hosting account. It should contain a link to cPanel.

And if that fails, ask your hosting provider to tell you or google 'access cPanel [my hosting provider]'.

The hosting provider I use (and recommend) is Siteground. To access cPanel via their client area, I go to **My Accounts > Go to cPanel**.

You're then presented with the cPanel screen.

Image 10-1 The cPanel interface in Siteground

At this point, you might panic. So many options! Databases! Joomla! Mail! Security! How on earth do you know where to start?

OK, grab yourself a paper bag and breathe into it for a few seconds. In the words of *The Hitchhiker's Guide to the Galaxy*, DON'T PANIC.

You only need to find the WordPress auto-installer. Ignore everything else. Just blank it out. Pretend it isn't there.

Calmer now? Good. Let's continue.

You should find a section called **Autoinstallers**. In that section you're looking for an icon with the word **WordPress** beneath it. If you can't find that, you'll need to use **Softaculous** instead.

Let me start by demonstrating the process with the dedicated WordPress installer.

INSTALLING WORDPRESS WITH THE WORDPRESS AUTO-INSTALLER

Click on the WordPress logo. This will take you to a set of screens for installing WordPress.

If the **Install** tab isn't already open, click on it.

Now complete the fields as below.

- **Version**: leave this as the default.
- **Protocol**: If you have SSL already set up for your site (some providers give you this when you register the domain), select **https://**. If not (or if in doubt), select **http://** (Note: SSL makes your site more secure and is covered in detail in Chapter 36).
- **Choose Domain**: If you have more than one domain registered, choose the one you want to use.
- **In Directory**: leave this blank.
- **Site Name**: Enter the name of your site. You can change this later.
- **Site Description**: Your tagline. Again, you can change this later.
- **Enable Multisite**: Leave this unchecked. Some auto-installers don't have this: don't worry if you can't see it.
- **Admin Username**: type in the username you want to use. Don't use *admin* as this isn't very secure. You can't change this so make sure it's what you intend to use forever.
- **Admin Password**: type in the password you want to use. Use something different from your username, with a few upper-case letters and numbers for extra security. You want to make it as hard as possible for people to get into your site. You can change your password later via the WordPress admin screens, to make it more secure.
- **Admin Email**: type in the email address you want to use for any emails relating to your site. This isn't publicly displayed.
- **Select Language**: Choose your language.
- **Select Plugins**: leave all of these unchecked (this will only be an option with some hosting providers: don't fret if it isn't there).
- **WordPress Starter**: Uncheck this (again, this is

specific to some hosting providers and you might not have it).

If there are any other options, just leave them unchecked. And ignore any advanced settings: you don't need to worry about them.

Once you've filled out the fields, click the **Install** button.

The auto-installer will take some time to do its thing and then you'll be taken to a screen with details of your new site. There will be a link to the site itself and a link to your dashboard.

Congratulations, you now have a WordPress site!

INSTALLING WORDPRESS WITH SOFTACULOUS

If your cPanel doesn't have a dedicated WordPress installer, you can use Softaculous instead. Follow these steps:

1. Click on the Softaculous icon in cPanel.
2. From the menu on the left, select **WordPress**.
3. Click the WordPress icon at the top of the screen.
4. Follow the steps in 'Installing WordPress with the WordPress Auto-installer' above.

In fact, the WordPress auto-installer is nothing more than a shortcut to the Softaculous installer. So the process is the same.

Once you've done that, you can follow the link to your shiny new site and start getting it ready.

'THE FAMOUS FIVE MINUTE INSTALL': DOING IT MANUALLY

Now for the brave folks. The strong at heart. The courageous types who aren't put off by the thought of (gulp) creating a database and (yikes) downloading and uploading some software.

You might be someone who'd rather take a bit more time to get themselves a clean WordPress installation without using an auto-installer. Or you might be unlucky, and have signed up for hosting that doesn't include an auto-installer.

Either way, this is how you do the WordPress 'famous five-minute install', so called because—you guessed it—it is supposed to take no more than five minutes.

This consists of four steps:

1. Download the WordPress software.
2. Create an empty database on your hosting account.
3. Upload the software.
4. Run through the setup process.

This is all supposed to take five minutes, but in my experience, it normally takes half an hour, especially if you haven't done it before. The exact way you do it will depend on your hosting provider and what kind of cPanel you have: follow the instructions at wp4writers.com/5minuteinstall, which are kept up to date.

Once you've followed those steps and you have your WordPress installation in place, you can log in. Congratulations! You now have a WordPress website.

THE WORDPRESS DASHBOARD

HURRAH!

The tricky and (let's face it) boring bit is out of the way. You've signed up for a hosting account, registered a domain, and installed WordPress.

From now on, the process of managing your website is very similar to managing a WordPress.com site. With one major difference: you can install as many plugins as you like from thousands of available options, and you have access to thousands of free themes, instead of just a few.

But the abundance of choice can be quite bewildering. With some many themes and plugins to choose from, just where do you start?

In the next few chapters of this book, I'll guide you through the process of getting your site set up. I'll help you choose a theme that fits your author brand, to find the plugins that will make your site fast, secure and engaging, and show you how to manage your site and keep it up to date.

Note: This chapter examines the WordPress.org dashboard. The WordPress.com dashboard is different - it's covered in Chapter 4.

THE MAIN DASHBOARD SCREEN

When you first log into your new site (squee! You have an author website), you'll be taken to the WordPress dashboard screen.

Accessing the WordPress Dashboard

When you create your site using an auto-installer, you'll be given the link to your dashboard. You'll probably also receive an email with a link. But in case you don't, the link to your admin screens (or dashboard) is *authorname.com/wp-admin*, where *authorname.com* is your domain name.

You might want to create a bookmark to this in your browser so you can easily find it again.

Image 11-1 The WordPress dashboard

The dashboard screen will include a number of dashboard widgets, which are likely to include:

- **Welcome to WordPress**: some useful tips and links.
- **At a Glance**: an overview of your site's content.

- **Quick Draft**: a widget that lets you quickly add a post.
- **Activity**: A list of recent activity including posts and comments.
- **WordPress Events and News**: news about WordPress.

These might differ depending on your hosting and your auto-installer—some auto-installers add an extra dashboard widget or two.

This is the main dashboard screen, but as you work on your site, you'll spend more time in other admin screens, such as the post editing screen.

Using the WordPress.com interface with WordPress.org

If you've worked with WordPress.com in the past and are familiar with that interface, you'll be pleased to know that you can activate the same admin screens by installing the free Jetpack plugin.

Jetpack makes WordPress.org work like WordPress.com but with all the extra benefits of WordPress.org, and it also gives you some of the features of WordPress.com like the community and social sharing.

To find out how to use Jetpack, see Chapter 16.

Let's take a look at each section of the dashboard in turn. You can access each of these via the admin menu on the left-hand side.

POSTS

The first and most important section of the WordPress admin is the Posts section.

Click on **Posts** in the admin menu and some more options will appear:

- **All Posts** displays a list of all your posts.
- **Add New** is where you create a new post.
- **Categories** lets you set categories for your posts, which you can then use to create sections for your blog. There's more about categories in Chapter 22.
- **Tags** gives you access to post tags, which are similar to categories but work differently. Find out more in Chapter 22.

Click on the **All Posts** link (or the **Posts** link above it) to see your existing posts. WordPress may have created a dummy post for you, or this may be empty (this will depend on your auto-installer).

We'll dive into posts in much more detail in Chapter 22, where you'll learn how to create and edit posts and assign categories and tags to them.

MEDIA

The next section of the admin screens is for managing your media —i.e. any files you upload to your site. These can include images, video, pdf files or even epub files.

The screens for managing media are:

- **Library**: a list of all your uploaded media.
- **Add New**: as you might imagine, the screen where you upload new media. You can also upload media straight to your posts and pages, which is what I do 99% of the time.

Media is covered in detail in Chapter 23.

PAGES

The pages admin screens are similar to the posts admin screens, except you don't have the option to assign categories and tags to pages. These screens are:

- **All Pages**: a list of existing pages.
- **Add New**: no prizes for guessing what this is for.

Pages and Posts: What's the Difference?

A Page is static content that doesn't change over time, such as your contact page or your 'About me' page. A post is an update, or a blog post.

Most of the content you'll be creating will be posts. Posts are listed on your blog page and they're what you'll be sharing with your audience and using to keep your site fresh.

COMMENTS

The admin screens for comments let you view and manage comments that visitors leave on your blog posts.

It's a good idea to include commenting in your posts, as it increases engagement and lets your readers contact you and give feedback on your posts. It can also encourage the development of a community of readers who talk to each other in the comments.

For more on comments, see Chapter 32.

APPEARANCE

Now we're getting into more intricate stuff.

If you click on **Appearance**, you'll see a bunch of available screens that you can use to modify the appearance of your site. These include:

- **Themes**: find and manage your theme—see Chapter 13.
- **Customize**: the Customizer lets you customize the look and feel of your site while being able to see how it looks. If you've used WordPress.com, this will be familiar.
- **Widgets**: these are snippets of content that you add to

your sidebar and/or footer. They include things like a list of your latest posts or a social media feed.

- **Menus**: use this screen to create a navigation menu for your site and add pages to it.
- **Theme Editor**: if this is available for your site, IGNORE IT. If I could write that in flashing pink letters with fairy lights garlanded over it, I would. It's important. This is a screen that lets you directly edit the code powering your theme. If you make changes to it, **you could break your site**. Most auto-installers deliberately remove access to it but if it's there for your site, leave well alone. (And if you do mess it up and need to restore your site, I hope you've skipped ahead to Chapter 35 and used a backup plugin.)

PLUGINS

Here's where you install and activate plugins for your site. You'll need plugins to make your site more secure and robust, and to add features like newsletter signups.

We'll be covering plugins in Chapter 15.

USERS

Use these screens to manage the users for your site. This includes you as a site admin and anyone else for whom you might grant access. There are five levels of user account:

- **Subscriber**: someone who follows your site and is notified by email when you publish something new.
- **Contributor**: someone who can write content but can't publish it (it needs to be approved by an editor or administrator).
- **Author**: can create and publish their own posts but can't edit anyone else's.

- **Editor**: Can create content and approve other people's posts.
- **Administrator**: Can create and publish all content and manage site settings. You're the site administrator because you created the site.

You might not need to add anyone else to your site, or you might have other members of your team who create or manage contact for you. Use the **Add User** screen to add a new user with the relevant level of access.

TOOLS

This menu gives you access to extra tools for managing your site. Some of these come out of the box (importing and exporting) but most will be added by plugins.

If you're migrating from WordPress.com or from another website platform, you can use the importer to import all of your content. See Chapter 19 for detailed instructions.

SETTINGS

Here's where you configure things like the way your home page works and the site title and tagline.

Chances are you'll only need to visit this section once, when you first set up your site, but it's reassuring to know it's there should you need to change anything in future.

For more on settings, see Chapter 14.

So that's the WordPress admin screens. You'll become more familiar with these as we work through the following chapters and you get your site set up.

So without further ado, let's start having some fun. It's time to start creating content for your site.

CREATING YOUR FIRST CONTENT

BEFORE YOU WORK on how your site looks, I recommend quickly creating a couple of posts and pages. That way, you've got some content to look at when you're testing out themes.

I'll cover creating posts and pages in more detail in Chapters 20-22, but for now, let's just quickly get a couple of each published.

Note: this is very similar to the process outlined for WordPress.com in Chapter 5. But some of the screens and buttons are slightly different. Over time, it's likely that the two systems will converge and WordPress.org will look more like WordPress.com. So if the screens you're seeing aren't the same as I'm describing, check out Chapter 5 and follow the instructions there.

CREATING A POST

There are two ways to create a post: either click the **+New** link in the admin toolbar at the top of the screen, or go to **Posts > Add New** in the admin menu.

You'll now see the blank screen for creating your post.

Start by typing in the post title. Then either hit **Return** on your keyboard or click into the box for your first paragraph. Just type as you normally would. Every time you hit **Return**, a new block will be created. Each block represents a paragraph of text. You can convert your paragraphs to lists, headings, or other text blocks, or you can create blocks for images or other media.

Blocks and post creation are covered in much more detail in Chapter 20; for now we're just creating a dummy post. Type whatever you fancy into the post (remember you can always delete this later).

Once you're happy with your post (remember, this is a dummy post; you'll spend longer crafting your exquisite tracts of literary loveliness later), click on the **Publish** button, which you'll find at the top right of the screen.

You'll be presented with a few pre-publish checks. These re really useful when you come to write 'proper' posts for your blog, as they help you check the post is ready before you publish it. But for now, don't fret. Just hit the **Publish** button again.

Now, repeat that to create your second post. To add another post, click the back arrow at the top left of the screen, and go to **Posts > Add New** or click that **+New** button in the top menu bar.

Add some content to your post (don't worry about what it is yet), and publish it.

Sorted!

CREATING A PAGE

Your site is also going to need a few pages. We're not going to create them all here, but you will need two to help you with setting up your menu and your home page settings.

To get started, create two pages: one called Home and one called Blog.

To create a page, go to **Pages > Add New** in the admin menu or click **+New > Page** in the admin bar. Give your page a title of *Home*. For the home page, type in some content (don't worry about what this is just yet, you can come back to it later). Click the **Publish** button to publish it, then click **Publish** again.

Now do the same for the 'Blog' page. To add another page, click the back arrow on the top left of the screen and click **Pages > Add New** (or **+New > Page**) again.

This time, leave the page empty. WordPress will automatically populate this page with your blog posts: you don't need to add anything.

Publish your empty page, and go back to the main menu by clicking the back arrow at the top left of the screen.

You now have two pages in your site.

Over time, you'll want to add more content to your site, of course. The process for doing this is the same for WordPress.com and for self-hosted WordPress. So skip on over to Chapter 17 if you want to know more. Or alternatively, keep on reading and get your site looking good.

TIME TO GET TWEAKING!

Tweaking the site and theme settings is much easier when you have some content on your site, as you can see what effect your changes will have on your content.

Now we've quickly created those two posts and two pages, let's move on to choosing a theme to reflect your author brand.

BRANDING YOUR SITE WITH A THEME

So you're happy to throw up a website and use the default theme: if it's good enough for thousands of others, its good enough for you.

Ahem. Go and stand in the corner for five minutes and think about how your website impacts on your author career.

Your website is part of your brand as an author. Now before you shout at me that branding is something that applies to big companies like McDonalds and Apple, stop to consider how brand might actually be just as important for authors.

YOU'RE A BRAND: LET YOUR WEBSITE REFLECT THAT

But I'm not a brand, you're saying. *I'm just me. I like to sit in my garret and create works of literary genius.*

Has it occurred to you that being someone who sits in a garret and creates works of literary genius may be your author brand?

Just as much as creating fast-paced thrillers that people can't put down might be? Or writing sci-fi adventures that are adored by people who miss Firefly?

The genre you write in and the style of your writing is part of your author brand.

So are your book covers. If you work with a cover designer (if you're with a publisher, that goes without saying, and if you're self-published I recommend it), then you'll have worked together to create a set of book covers that have something in common and label your books as being written by you. In other words: you've created a brand.

Your author brand isn't just visual. Your authorial voice is part of your brand. Your social media presence. The way you dress at writing conventions. Anything you do in public that tells people something about the kind of writer you are: that's your brand.

It's not corporate, or cheesy: it's designed to help readers identify what you write and whether that's something they'd like.

Having a coherent author brand will help you sell books. Don't shy away from it.

So it needs to carry through to your website. The theme that you choose and the way you configure it will reflect your brand and have some consistency with your book covers.

IDENTIFYING YOUR BRAND

So you're prepared to accept that you need a brand, but you haven't the first idea what your brand might be.

Maybe you don't have any book covers yet and you're creating a website in anticipation of publishing your first book or getting a book deal. (Good for you: it pays to get yourself a website as early as possible.)

Maybe your publisher has given your books wildly different covers and you have no idea how this links to any sort of brand. (You'd be surprised how often publishers do this.)

Maybe you've been published by multiple publishers and they've covered your books in very different ways.

Or maybe your publisher has given your books covers that you can't stand and don't see as part of your brand. (This does happen, but remember that your brand isn't about what you like: it's about what communicates with your readers.)

If you recognize any of these, it's up to you to decide what your brand is going to be. It might not be based on your existing covers.

And if you do already have a coherent brand from your covers or your publicity materials: even better. You've got a starting point.

Grab a piece of paper and a pen (I'll wait). Make notes on the following:

- What genre do you write in?
- What is the tone of your writing? Humorous? Suspenseful? Gory? Educational?
- What colors, fonts and imagery are used on your existing book covers?
- What branding do other authors in your genre use? (I'm not telling you to copy them, just to take some cues from what's going on in your genre.)

Once you've got a note of these, ask yourself:

- What colors should I use on my website?
- Will the overall tone be dark, or light?
- What kind of fonts do I need? (If you can use the same fonts from your covers that's great, but I'll show you how to find similar ones if you can't.)
- What tone of writing do I need to use for my content?
- What images should I use? Will these be photographic, or illustrations?

All of this will be a constant work in progress, as your author brand will evolve over time (especially if you're starting out). But answering these questions will help you find the best WordPress theme for your site and to customize it so it reflects your brand.

HELP! THERE ARE TOO MANY THEMES TO CHOOSE FROM

I feel your pain.

At time of writing, clicking **Latest** in the WordPress theme directory gives me 7,106 free themes. And that's just the latest ones.

How the heck do you choose between them?

OK. Let's take a deep breath and identify a way through the maze.

There are two approaches to finding a suitable WordPress theme:

- Find one with a design that reflects your brand.
- Find one you can customize to reflect your brand.

Let's take a look at how you'd go about each.

Free Themes vs Premium Themes

In this book, I'm going to focus entirely on free themes. I believe that it's possible to get yourself a free theme that will make your author website look great. However if you do decide to buy a premium theme, you can find details of providers recommended by the folks behind WordPress at wp4writers.com/premiumthemes.

FINDING A THEME THAT REFLECTS YOUR BRAND

This could take you a while, but will save time tweaking the theme. The downside is that if you decide you need to change your design in the future, it could be difficult .

Do I need to pick a theme designed for author websites?

There's a very short answer to this: no.

Your theme is about the way your site looks. That will be unique to you as an author, and it's unlikely that there's a one-size-fits-all theme that can meet every author's needs.

So resist the temptation to limit yourself to a theme designed just for authors. Instead, focus on finding one that reflects your brand.

INSTALLING AND ACTIVATING A THEME (DON'T WORRY IF IT LOOKS AWFUL)

Right, let's roll our sleeves up and get to work installing a theme.

To install a theme, click the **Appearance** link in the admin menu. Click the **Add New** button.

This will take you to a screen with lots of themes listed. There are three tabs: Featured, Popular, Latest and Favorites. Take a look at them all and see if you can find anything you like.

Alternatively, search for what you need using the search box at the top. Use words that relate to your brand, such as the color you want to use, or the mood. (Or both!) You can also search for terms like *customize* to get a theme you can customize, or be more specific and type something like *customize fonts* or *customize colors*.

When you find a theme you like the look of, you can preview it by clicking the **Preview** button below its image. Beware: the preview functionality isn't brilliant, and it may show you something that doesn't look too hot.

I find that what works better is to try a few themes out and preview them in the Customizer. You access this by going to **Appearance > Customize**.

At the top of the customization sidebar on the left, it'll tell you what theme is currently active (probably the default theme, which is nowhere near as good as many of the other themes you can download). Click the **Change** button next to its name and then select the **Word-Press.org themes** radio button to see a range of available themes.

Now you can use the search field at the top of the screen to search themes using your own criteria, and you can also use the **Filter themes** button at the top right to filter the themes and find a good one that way.

I won't lie: there are so many themes that finding a good one can take a while. You can find my recommendations for themes that are suitable for authors at wp4writers.com/themes. These are themes that include a clickable banner image and customization options that will help you make your site your own.

Because you already added a couple of posts and pages (you did, didn't you?), you will be able to see how the theme looks with your content. Even so, you'll probably need to give it some tweaks to get it looking the way you want it to.

THEME CONFIGURATION (NOW THAT'S BETTER)

You can customize the theme in the Customizer before you activate it, which gives you the opportunity to see how good it can look without committing yourself.

Every theme will have different customization options: experiment with the options in the Customizer menu, trying out different changes until you're happy the theme looks the way you want it to. If you decide you can't get the theme looking quite how you want, you can always try another theme.

When you are happy with the theme and your customizations, please, *please,* ***please*** don't forget to click the **Publish** button at the top of the screen. If you leave the Customizer without doing this, none of your changes will be saved.

And if you're experimenting with a number of themes, it's a good idea to make notes as you go along. Keep notes on which themes you tested, what you liked and didn't like about them, and the customizations you made. There's every chance that after testing ten themes you decide you prefer the second one you looked at. If you can't remember what that was or how you customized it when testing, it could be very frustrating.

Don't forget you can come back to the Customizer at any time and make more tweaks. You might find that once you've added more content to your site, you want things to look a little different. Or you might decide to make changes to your branding when you have a new book out or you or your publisher changes the covers on your books. This is why it's a good idea to use a theme that includes robust customization options.

HELPING PEOPLE GET AROUND WITH A NAVIGATION MENU

Now you have your theme set up, you'll need to set up a navigation menu.

Go to **Appearance > Menus**.

Your auto-installer may already have set up a navigation menu for you, in which case you select that and start editing it.

If there isn't already a menu created, just type in the name you want to give your menu and click the **Create Menu** button.

Now you can add items to your menu from the list on the left. You can add the following:

- **Pages**: it's a good idea to add most of your pages to the main menu.
- **Posts**: normally you wouldn't add posts as they'll show up in your 'Blog' page instead (or maybe on your home page).
- **Categories**: add the main categories for your blog posts if you want, to encourage people to browse. This is most relevant for a nonfiction site.
- **Custom Links**: these are links to other parts of your site or to other websites. For example you might want to include a link to your Amazon author page.

To create a custom link, select the **Custom Links** box on the left, then type in the URL you want the link to go to, or copy it from another window in your browser (you'll find it at the top of the screen when you're on that page). Then type in the text you want to use for the link text and click the **Add to Menu** button. So you could set up a 'Buy' link for example, linking to your Amazon author page.

Once you have all the items in your menu that you want, you can reorder them. Just drag them up and down to put them in the order you want. You can also put menu items underneath each other by dragging them to the side, so they appear in a hierarchical list.

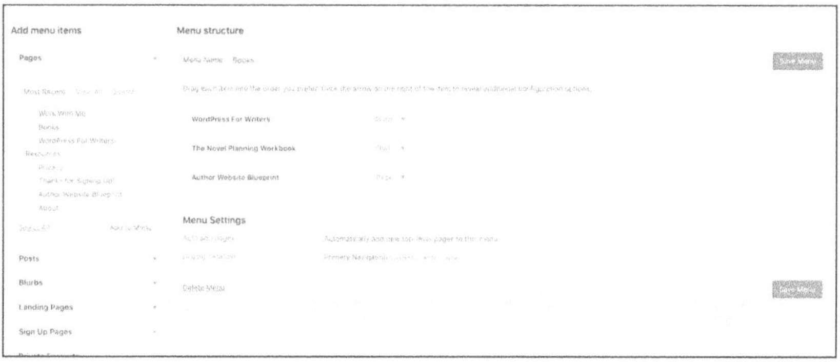

Image 13-1 Hierarchical menu

And when you're happy with your menu, click the **Save Menu** button to save it.

Your menu still won't actually appear in your site, though (frustrating, I know).

To fix this, look beneath the menu items you've added and you'll find one or more checkboxes for menu positions in the theme. The names of these (and the number of them) varies between themes but you'll probably have one called **Primary** or something like it. Check the box for that.

You can also edit and create menus via the Customizer, and if you like to see a preview of your menu before you save it, you might like to do that instead.

Click on **Appearance > Customize** and then select the **Menus** option. Select the menu you want to edit or click the **Create New Menu** button to create a new one.

To add items to the menu, click the **Add Items** button and then select the items from the options that will appear to the right of the menu editing pane. You can then drag the menu items around in the menu in the same way you would on the Menus screen.

When you're happy with your menu, don't forget to click **Publish** at the top of the screen.

Help! I changed my theme and my menu disappeared.

Don't panic. This is entirely normal and your menu isn't lost.

Each theme has its own slot for navigation menus, and they'll be different across themes. So all you need to do is tell WordPress where in your theme you want your menu to appear. Go to the Customizer or the Menus screen, select your main menu (it's still there, phew), and check the checkbox for the location where you want it to appear. It will magically reappear.

GO CRAZY WITH WIDGETS

Now you have your menu set up, it's time to add some widgets.

These are snippets of content that you put in the sidebar and/or footer of your theme. They're useful for links to your latest blog posts, tag clouds, newsletter signups (see Chapter 27) and lots more.

The widget areas you have available to you will depend on your theme. To find out what there is, either go to **Appearance > Widgets** or **Appearance > Customize** and select the **Widgets** option.

Here you can select from a range of widgets and add them to the widget areas that are provided in your theme.

There are a bunch of widgets that come with WordPress out of the box, such as a tag cloud, a list of your latest posts, a list of your categories, a custom menu (useful for items you don't have space for in your main menu), some text or an image.

You can also add more widgets with plugins. So if you have the Jetpack plugin, for example, you have access to all the widgets from WordPress.com, such as a Facebook feed widget. A mailing list plugin will often give you a widget you can use to get signups to your mailing list.

I like to add the following widgets to my sidebar:

- A text widget taking people to my newsletter sign up page (see Chapter 30 for instructions on setting this up).
- A list of recent posts.
- A list of the categories in my blog.

I also like to add social media feeds to the footer of my site, because they can take up too much space in the sidebar.

But your theme might not have widget areas in both the sidebar and the footer, maybe because it's got a full-width design. Or it might have extra widgets such as home page widgets (which can be great for directing people to other parts of the site). It'll all depend on your theme.

It's entirely up to you which widgets you add. Spend some time experimenting with some widgets and remember, you can always come back and change them or add more in the future. With your website, nothing is set in stone.

Can I add a widget to my posts or pages?

Yes, you can. To do this, start editing the post or page, then add a new block and select the **Widget** block type. Choose which widget you want to add and you're all set. This can be a great way of adding custom content to your home page; I use the Latest Posts widget to add a list of my latest blog posts under the text in my home page at rachelmcwrites.com.

So now you have your theme set up. You've picked a theme that's right for your brand, customized it, and added widgets and a menu. Your work isn't done, I'm afraid. Time to tweak your site settings.

SITE SETTINGS: MAKING THINGS HUM

ONCE YOU HAVE some content in place and you've configured your theme, your menu and your widgets, you need to spend a little time configuring your site settings.

In this chapter, I'll take you through the settings that are available to you and show you how to configure them.

I know this isn't the most exciting prospect in the world (you're sneaking off to watch cat videos again, aren't you?), but the good news is that you can do this once and then forget about it.

WHAT ARE SITE SETTINGS?

Site settings are instructions to WordPress on how your site as a whole should work. They don't relate to individual posts or pages, but instead to the website as a whole.

You can use them to add metadata (data about data) to your site or to tweak the way the site looks to visitors.

Let's work through the settings screens.

TWEAKING GENERAL SETTINGS

To access the general settings, click on **Settings** in the admin menu.

Here you can edit the following:

- **Site Title**: Normally your author name, although some nonfiction authors prefer to use a title that's related to their subject matter.
- **Tagline**: Your strapline. For my nonfiction site, it's *Writing, Websites and Productivity*. For my fiction site, it's *Thrillers That Make You Think*. This is a short phrase that tells visitors more about you and your writing.
- **WordPress address**: The address of your site. Leave this as it is.
- **Site address**: The address you want people to use for your site. You should normally leave this as it is, unless you have another domain name pointing to your site and want to use that instead. If so, get advice from your hosting provider on making it work.
- **Email address**: Your email address. This is where all notifications will be sent (e.g. form submissions and security alerts).
- **Membership**: Check this if you want to encourage people to subscribe to your site and get notifications when you add a new post. You can also do this using the Jetpack plugin, which gives you access to the WordPress.com community (which is what I recommend). I wouldn't bother checking this: the functionality provided by Jetpack is better.
- **New User Default Role**: Leave this on **Subscriber**.
- Site language, time zone and date settings: Depending on your auto-installer, these will either already be set to your own time zone, or they'll default to something else. If you want to adjust them, this is where you do it.

Once you've made any changes, click the **Save Changes** button.

CONFIGURING WRITING SETTINGS

Now to the next settings screen. This one is a little less dull.

The only setting on this screen that I'd edit is the **Default Post Category** item. This will default to **Uncategorized**, meaning that if you publish a post and forget to give it any categories, it'll be marked as 'Uncategorized'. Not very helpful, so once you have your categories set up, I'd change this to the category you're least worried about accidentally publishing posts under.

Don't forget if you do accidentally publish a post without adding categories, you can always go back and edit the post in question to change its categories.

After making any changes, click the **Save Changes** button (do you really need me to keep telling you to do that?).

CONFIGURING READING SETTINGS

The Reading settings screen is where you tell WordPress whether your home page will be a list of your blog posts or a static page (see Chapter 12).

You can also tweak the number of posts showing on an archive page. Ignore the settings relating to showing full text or a summary, as most of the themes I've worked with will override this anyway.

Finally, you can discourage search engines from indexing your site—useful when you're first setting up the site and don't want people stumbling across it yet. Just remember to change this setting back again when you go live, or Google will never send people to your site.

If you can't find your site in a search.

If you ever find that you can't find your own site on

Google, or you aren't getting any traffic via search engines, then the culprit could be this setting.

Go to **Settings > Reading** and see if you've forgotten to uncheck the box. If you install an SEO plugin, it will repeatedly warn you if this is the case.

CONFIGURING DISCUSSION SETTINGS

The Discussion screen lets you configure commenting on your site. This is where you decide if you're going to allow comments or not.

I think allowing comments is a very good idea, as it gives your readers a chance to get in touch. See Chapter 32 for more about comments.

MAKING YOUR PERMALINKS PRETTY

Depending on the way your auto-installer configured your site, you may find that the URLs for your posts are less than pretty.

Let's say you've published a post called 'My Latest Book'. Its URL should be something like *yourwebsite.com/my-latest-book*.

But you've checked it in your browser, and it's showing up as *yourwebsite.com/?p=456*.

Eurrgh.

You can fix this in the Permalinks settings screen. Simply open the screen and select the **Post name** option, then click **Save Changes**. Go back to your post, refresh the screen, and it'll all work as it should.

If you ever find you can't access a page in your site, try going to this screen and then going back to your page and refreshing. This flushes the permalinks (you don't need to worry about what that means) and tells your browser what it should be showing. It sometimes happens after you install a plugin that adds a new post type to your site.

ADDING AND EDITING USERS

Another thing you might need to do is add or edit the users in your site.

To do this, go to the **Users** menu item. This will give you a list of the users currently registered.

The chances are there's only one user: you. But here you can add extra users, for example if you have an editor who works with you on your content, or another contributor to your blog.

As the person who created and owns the website, you will have the top level of user account: you will be an administrator. If you add new users, you can give them one of four levels of access:

- Editor: can add and publish content and edit other people's content but can't access site settings.
- Author: can create and publish their own posts.
- Contributor: can create posts but can't publish them. Instead, an editor or administrator will need to do this. As a freelance writer I work on lots of sites with this level of access.
- Subscriber: can view the site but can't add or edit content.

You might find that you have additional user roles if you've installed a plugin that includes them, such as an e-commerce plugin, that might add something like 'Shop Manager'.

In the Users section of the admin screens, you can also edit your own details using the **Your Profile** link in the admin menu. Here you can edit your screen name, your email address and personal details, and you can change your password.

As an administrator, you can also edit some of the details for other users by going to **Users** and clicking the **Edit** link under the username.

Well done! You got through the really boring bit. Now it's time to add some extra functionality to your site, with plugins.

15

ADDING THE TOP FIVE AUTHOR PLUGINS

You're making progress! You now have a site that's branded the way you want it to be and has its first content.

But you're not done yet.

One of the greatest features of self-hosted WordPress is the vast range of plugins. These add extra functionality to your site: anything from a call-to-action button to a fully-fledged store.

You might have specific functionality you want to add to your site, but first, I want you to install the essential plugins your site needs if it's going to be effective, robust and secure (bossy, aren't I?).

So let's get started by identifying the five plugins every author site needs.

TOP 5 PLUGINS FOR AUTHOR SITES

The five plugins I believe every author site should have will give your site the following functionality:

- Linking to your mailing list
- Keeping your site backed up

- Search Engine Optimization (SEO)
- Security
- Social media and other WordPress.com features.

These are important plugins to set up before you start creating large amounts of content.

Mailing list signups will be one of the primary functions of your website and without it, your website isn't working as hard for you as it might.

Backups and security will protect your site from attacks and make it possible for you to restore a clean version of your site if it should be hacked or stop working for any reason.

SEO is essential if you want people to find your site. This is especially important for nonfiction authors: SEO will be one of your most important tools for attracting potential readers.

And finally, installing the Jetpack plugin will give you access to a host of features that you'd have if you were using WordPress.com. These include social media sharing, site stats and the community of WordPress.com users.

INSTALLING AND ACTIVATING A PLUGIN

Let's start by installing and activating one of those plugins.

In your site admin, go to **Plugins > Add New**.

In the search box, type in *All In One SEO*.

You'll be presented with a list of plugins, one of which is All In One SEO Pack.

Click the **Install Now** button. WordPress will install the plugin.

Congratulations, you've installed your first plugin. We'll come back to plugin configuration in a moment. But first, let's get the other four plugins installed.

Repeat the steps above for the following:

- The Wordfence plugin
- The Jetpack plugin

- The Updraft Plus plugin
- The plugin for your mailing list provider (which plugin you install will depend on your provider).

Everyone tells me to install SEO by Yoast, but Rachel, you're telling me to install the All In One SEO Pack plugin. Why?

Good question. SEO by Yoast is the most popular SEO plugin, but I think it has flaws.

Firstly, it has a habit of making my sites crash when I update it. I don't want that happening to you.

And secondly, when you do install it, it triggers a load of popups nagging you to configure the plugin or learn more about it. These get in the way of working on your site.

If you do want to install SEO by Yoast, then go ahead. But please don't be surprised if it makes your site hang after an update, or if it makes you want to scream at those popups.

For now, let's get the two most important plugins configured: backups and security. You can come back to the others later if you want, or configure them after these two.

You'll find more details about all of the plugins later in the book:

- Mailing list: Chapter 30
- Backups: Chapter 35
- SEO: Chapter 25
- Security: Chapter 36
- Social media: Chapter 16

But first, let's make sure your site is secure and that it's being backed up regularly.

MAKING PLUGINS WORK HOW YOU WANT THEM TO: CONFIGURATION

Before you can get your plugins working the way you want to, you need to configure them. Let's do it.

CONFIGURING YOUR SECURITY PLUGIN

First, the Wordfence security plugin.

Go to the **Plugins** screen, find Wordfence, and click **Activate**.

You'll be taken to a screen asking you where security alerts should be sent. Type in your email address. Select whether or not you'd like to be added to the Wordfence mailing list (it will make no difference to you receiving your own security alerts), check the terms & conditions box and then click the **Continue** button.

The next screen will prompt you for a Premium Key. You'll only have one of these if you've paid for the premium version of the software. Click on **No thanks**.

You'll be taken back to the plugins page. If you look at your admin menu on the left, you'll see an extra item called **Wordfence**. Click on that to be taken to the Wordfence dashboard.

The plugin will take you through a few guidance popups. Click your way through that to get rid of them (am I the only person who never pays any attention to these things?). If you want, you can spend some time looking through the settings screens and tweaking them. But I'd advise leaving well alone. The default settings are what works best for the majority of sites so unless you're a website security expert, then it's safest to leave things as they are.

If your site is compromised in any way in the future, the plugin will send you an email, with help on fixing the problem.

If your site should be compromised in a big way, however, the best thing to do is restore it from a backup. Which brings me to the next plugin…

CONFIGURING BACKUPS

It's very (very, very, veryveryveryvery) important to configure automatic backups for your site.

Your hosting provider probably tells you they back up your hosting account on a regular basis, and in theory this means that they could restore your site for you if there was a problem.

But what your hosting provider probably won't be so quick to tell you is that their backups aren't guaranteed. Every hosting provider I've ever worked with has a clause in its terms and conditions saying you shouldn't rely on their backups. This means you can't sue them if their backup fails.

Luckily, once you've installed and configured a backup plugin, you can leave it to do its work behind the scenes. And it's only if you need to restore your site in future that you'll need to look at it again.

It's very rare that you need to do this. In the last ten years I've created dozens of sites, and I've only twice had to restore any of them from a backup. The second time, I got an email from someone who'd visited my website and found it had been hacked. It was displaying some indecipherable text in Arabic and playing a tune that was supposed to be ominous. Unfortunately I was on a camping trip at the time (it's as if the hackers knew), but I made my excuses to my family, found the nearest Starbucks and restored my site from a backup taken before it had been breached. If I hadn't had my backup plugin running, I would have been stuck. And that would have been goodbye to my vacation!

As you're only going to be running one site, and you're going to keep it constantly updated (aren't you?), then it's unlikely that something like this will happen to you. But if it does, your backups will keep you safe.

Anyway, you're thinking. *Stop waffling on about backups and show me how to get them set up.*

Sorry. Here goes.

Go to your Plugins screen, find the Updraft Plus plugin and click **Activate** (is this becoming familiar yet?).

The plugin will activate and you'll see a popup. Click the **Press here to start!** button.

You'll be taken to the backup settings screen (which is at **Settings > UpdraftPlus Backups**). Ignore any popups that appear and click on the **Settings** tab at the top. This is where you configure your automated backups.

Let's work through the screen:

- **Files backup schedule**: select how often you want this to happen. It makes sense to have the same frequency for backups as you will have for adding new content to your site. So if you plan to blog every week, select **Weekly**.
- **Database backup schedule**: Choose the same as for Files backup schedule.
- **Remote storage**: select the remote storage option you'll use. If you have an account with a service like Dropbox or Google Drive, it makes sense to use that (I go into this in more detail in Chapter 35). If you don't have anything like that, just select **Email**.

Now scroll down to the bottom of the screen (you can leave all the other settings on the defaults) and click the **Save Changes** button.

If you selected a remote storage option, you'll be given a link to authorize your account. Follow the instructions to link your remote storage to your website and have backup files sent there. This will save you having to manage emailed backup files and make sure you store them somewhere.

Your site will now be backed up automatically on a regular basis. If you ever need to restore your site, go to **Settings > Updraft-Plus Backups > Backup/Restore**. Select the most recent backup that you know to be clean and follow the instructions to restore it. I hope you never have to use this, but it's good to know it's there.

KEEPING PLUGINS UP TO DATE

You now have your first plugins installed.

Plugins are occasionally updated by their developers. This might be to keep them compatible with a new version of WordPress, to add new features or to fix a bug.

Whatever the reason, it's a good idea to keep your plugins up to date. You should diarize to check your site on a regular basis (every month is realistic) and run any updates.

Before you update your plugins, always run a backup first. With the Updraft Plus plugin installed, you do this by going to **Settings > UpdraftPlus Backups > Backup/Restore** and clicking the **Backup Now** button.

This means that if the updates cause any problems on your site, you can restore it to the previous version. However it's very rare for plugins to cause problems and you shouldn't find yourself having to do this.

To update your plugins, go to the Plugins screen. Any plugin that needs updating will have a message telling you so. Simply click on **Update** and WordPress will update the plugin for you. Work down the screen doing this with every plugin that needs updating.

Once you've finished, go to your website's front end (i.e. the site itself and not the admin screens) and check everything's working as it should. If there are any problems, you might need to restore a backup or check the website for the plugin to find out if there's a fix. You can find a link to the site or page for each plugin next to it in the **Plugins** screen.

Updating isn't just for plugins!

As well as your plugins, you'll also need to keep your theme updated.

The process is the same as for plugins, but you access it by going to **Appearance > Themes**. Alternatively you can update both themes and plugins at **Dashboard > Updates**.

Updates are covered in more detail, including what to do if one goes wrong and how to automate them, in Chapter 37.

ADDING MORE PLUGINS

Your site is well on the way to being ready to go. But it's entirely possible that you'll have other plugins you want to add.

If you do need to add extra functionality, I strongly recommend using free plugins that you can get via the **Plugins > Add New** screen. All of these plugins have been tested and you can be confident that they'll be compatible with the latest version of WordPress (if they aren't, you'll see a warning) and that they are well-coded.

If you can't find what you need, then you might decide to buy a premium plugin. You can find out about recommended providers of premium plugins at wp4writers.com/premiumthemes.

A word of warning: don't be tempted to download free WordPress plugins from anywhere other than the WordPress plugin directory (i.e. the plugins you access via your dashboard). If a reputable developer wants to make a plugin available for free, they will upload it to the official directory, and submit it to the testing that involves.

If a developer decides to bypass that process, but isn't charging for the plugin, then ask yourself why they're doing it? There's a very good chance the plugin could contain malicious code.

So to sum up, only get your themes from one of two locations:

- Free themes from the official WordPress plugin directory.
- Premium themes from reputable providers.

The same applies to themes.
Follow this advice, and your site will be more secure.

Above I was a bit of a tease. I told you to install the Jetpack plugin, gave you hints as to its general awesomeness, then left it alone. Time to fix that: in the next chapter, you'll create a little bit of Word-Press.com goodness on your WordPres.org site, with probably my favorite plugin.

16

LOVE WORDPRESS.COM? HAVE THE BEST OF BOTH WORLDS WITH JETPACK

So you've switched from WordPress.com to WordPress.org, and you're feeling a little bereft.

Maybe you're missing the community of bloggers. Maybe you wish you could automatically share all your new content via social media. Or maybe it's the interface you wish you could have back.

Fear not: I have good news for you.

You can get yourself all the features of WordPress.com on your WordPress.org site with a free plugin: Jetpack.

WHY RECREATE WORDPRESS.COM ON A WORDPRESS.ORG SITE?

Good question. After all, if you're a fan of WordPress.com, then why not stick with that platform?

But by getting yourself a self-hosted site and installing Jetpack, you get the best of both worlds.

You get:

- A website on your own hosting, meaning you're not beholden to the company that runs WordPress.com.

- Access to thousands of free themes and plugins.
- The ability to use your own domain without paying extra.
- The ability to link your website to all the major mailing list providers.
- Access to the WordPress.com community.
- The choice between using the WordPress.com and WordPress.org admin screens (although over time I see WordPress.org's admin screens getting more and more like those at WordPress.com).
- The social media and other features of WordPress.com.

So when it comes to WordPress, you can have your cake and eat it.

Let's take a look at how you activate and configure Jetpack.

ACTIVATING JETPACK AND LINKING IT TO WORDPRESS.COM

You should have already installed Jetpack while following the previous chapter.

Help! How do I install the plugin?

If you skipped straight to this chapter because you love WordPress.com so much, then never fear.

Go to **Plugins > Add New**. Type *Jetpack* into the search bar. **Jetpack by WordPress.com** will appear at the beginning of a list of plugins. Click the **Install** button and you're done.

Now you're all caught up.

To activate Jetpack, go to the **Plugins** screen. Find the Jetpack plugin and click the **Activate** link.

Jetpack will now take you through the setup process. In the first screen, click the **Set up Jetpack** button.

The next step is to either log in to your existing WordPress.com account or to create a new one. Which you need to do will depend on whether you're migrating from an old WordPress.com site or settings things up from scratch.

If you already have a WordPress.com account, log in to it and click the **Approve** button to authorize the link.

If you don't have an account, click the button to create a new account and follow the steps provided. You'll find out more about setting up a WordPress.com account in Chapter 4. After setting up your account, click the button to approve the link between it and your website.

WordPress will take you through some setup screens (including ones designed to encourage you to buy a premium plan). Skip all of the screens and don't sign up for a premium plan—with a self-hosted site, you don't need it. Just click on the **Start with Free** button, which is conveniently below all the big boxes for premium plans and much smaller than them.

You'll now be taken back to the Jetpack dashboard, where you can start configuring the plugin.

MIGRATING CONTENT FROM WORDPRESS.COM

If you previously had a WordPress.com website and you want to migrate all the posts and pages into your shiny new self-hosted site, you can.

WordPress comes with an importer tool that lets you import content not only from WordPress.com but also from other services like Blogger.

Find out how to do it in Chapter 19.

JETPACK SETTINGS AND FEATURES

The Jetpack settings are very similar to the settings for WordPress.com, which are covered in detail in Chapters 4-7.

But the way you access them is a little different.

To get at your Jetpack settings, go to **Jetpack > Settings**. (Did you guess that? Well done you.) This will give you access to the following free features (I'm not including the premium ones as any you might need can be accessed via other free plugins):

- Performance improvements
- Carousel slideshows.
- The WordPress.com toolbar.
- Composing options.
- Custom content types: testimonials and portfolios.
- Theme enhancements including infinite scroll (do **not** activate the Jetpack mobile theme as your own theme will do a much better job on mobile devices).
- Social sharing (my personal favorite).
- Commenting via WordPress.com and social media accounts (another favorite).
- Subscriptions by other WordPress.com users.
- Related posts.
- Downtime monitoring and plugin auto updates.

To find out more about these features, head on over to the section of this book on WordPress.com. There you can learn how to get the most from WordPress.com features and how to really get the benefit of having WordPress.com with WordPress.org.

So that's WordPress.org, or at least how to get it set up.

In the next section of the book, we're going to get into the nuts and bolts of running your website. It's time to add some content.

V

CREATING CONTENT FOR YOUR SITE

CONTENT MARKETING WITH WORDPRESS

OK, so your site is set up on either WordPress.com or Word-Press.org. It's looking great, you've got plugins installed (if you're on WordPress.org) and you're ready to go.

Now for the fun part.

I mean, you're a writer, right? This is what you're good at.

(If you aren't looking forward to this bit more than you did the site configuration, you might want to consider a career change—they're always looking for WordPress developers.)

It's time to start bandying around another bit of yucky marketing speak that will make your flesh crawl: Content Marketing.

WHAT IS CONTENT MARKETING?

Before you throw this book at the wall in disgust at its utter crass-ness, hear me out.

Content marketing isn't a dirty word (two words, but you catch my drift).

It needn't be scuzzy, or manipulative.

It isn't about clickbaity articles with no real substance.

No. Content marketing is about writing.

That sounds a bit better, huh?

Content marketing is about producing content (which can be written but could also be audio, images or video) that will help to sell you as an author.

Why am I saying that content marketing will sell you, and not your books?

Well, that's because you don't want to be scuzzy.

Imagine two possible articles I could write for my blog:

- Why *WordPress for Writers* Will Skyrocket Your Author Career.
- How to Choose Between WordPress.com and WordPress.org.

The two articles have a very different feel, just from looking at the titles. The first is very sales-y, and focused on pushing my book. The second is aimed at helping readers with a relevant problem.

Which would you be more likely to read?

I predict that the second article would be much more popular. It's designed to help people answer a specific question. It's not pushy. It's not asking the reader to give me something (cash for their copy of the book). Instead it's giving them something (free advice).

Writing lots of helpful posts like the second one will help me build a reputation among people who visit the site. (Which is why I've been doing it!)

If you write regular content for your site which is relevant to your books, engaging for your audience, and well-written, then it will enhance your reputation. It will encourage people to come back again, and to sign up for your mailing list.

And then once they're on your mailing list, you can keep engaging them with great content and let them know when you've got a book out.

It all sounds like a lot of hard work, right? Well, it is. But building a successful and sustainable author career is also a lot of hard work.

Content marketing can help you reach new readers, especially if you write nonfiction.

But is it also relevant for the fiction authors out there?

I WRITE FICTION: CONTENT MARKETING ISN'T FOR ME! (OR IS IT?)

Yeah, yeah, you're thinking, shaking your head. *I write novels. Who wants to read my blog about how I get up every day, stroke my cat, sip at a coffee, and bang out two thousand words?*

You'd be surprised.

HOW ABOUT PUBLISHING FICTION ON YOUR BLOG?

Your updates don't have to be blog posts.

How about publishing short stories on your website, or novel extracts? I imagine you've got a number of short stories sitting in a drawer somewhere. Why not bring them out into the light of day, and give them an audience?

Kristine Katherine Rusch is an established author in multiple genres, who publishes a new short story to her blog every Monday (wp4writers.com/rusch). She reports a spike in website traffic on those days and clearly has a readership that wants to read those stories.

I've published my own stories on my fiction blog and find that they can be the posts that get the most engagement.

If you're nervous of putting your stories out there and worry that they might not be good enough, don't: if you're going to be a professional writer, you need to be read.

What about if you don't have stories to publish? How about serializing your novel as you write it?

This may seem counterintuitive (surely no one will pay for it if it's on your website?) but can help boost visibility for your book. Andy Weir, the author of *The Martian*, was about to give up on hopes of being published but instead, he decided to publish his book on his website as he wrote it. It found an enthusiastic audience, was then self-published, became a Hollywood movie and…well, the rest is history.

Now I'm not saying that by serializing your novel on your website you're going to be the next Andy Weir. But it could certainly help you find readers.

WHAT ELSE COULD YOU WRITE?

And your posts don't have to be limited to fiction. There are other things your readers will be interested in knowing more about:

- Character bios.
- Tidbits on your story worlds.
- Anecdotes about your writing process.
- Musings on what you'll write next (even better if you ask readers what they'd like you to write next).
- Updates on your research trips (with photos).
- Information about the subject of your stories (so if you write Regency fiction, engage your readers with interesting facts about the Regency period).
- Snippets from fellow authors in the same or similar genres. One of the beta readers for this book, Heide Goody, told me how she and her co-author Iain Grant put some book-related questions to other authors, and the shares by the other authors meant that these were some of the most popular posts on their blog (wp4writers.com/goody).

There are plenty of things you could be writing about, and engaging your readers with.

But I want to spend my time writing my novel, not my blog!

Yup. I get that. Devoting time to your work in progress is the most important thing any writer can do.

But that's where a bit of creativity can help.

Are there things you've already created during the process of writing, that you could publish on your blog? Character bios, notes on your story world, historical research? And of course, the story itself?

All of this gives you material you can use, without having to start from scratch.

...AND IF BLOGGING REALLY ISN'T FOR YOU...

...you don't have to do it.

Uh-huh.

If you hate the thought of blogging. If it makes you want to throw this book onto the floor and stamp on it (please don't, particularly if you're reading on your Kindle). If you're already struggling to find the time to write your goddamn novel and can't possibly squeeze anything else in.

You don't have to write blog posts. Give yourself a break. Come back to it later in your career, when you have more time.

Or don't.

It's up to you. This is your website, your audience, and your career.

If you think blogging, or publishing fiction online, is something you could do, then it can have real benefits.

But if you really, really don't want to do it—don't.

I WRITE NON-FICTION: GIMME THAT CONTENT MARKETING JUICE

OK. So I've just told you you don't have to blog.

But you're a nonfiction author. So you can forget everything I just said.

People find nonfiction books differently from how they find fiction. They're often looking for something to help them solve a problem.

If you want to learn how to write better English, you might buy *Grammar Girl's Quick And Dirty Tips for Better Writing*. If you want to simplify your home, you might buy *The Life-Changing Magic of Tidying*. If you want to get ahead in business, you might buy *The Seven Habits of Highly Effective People*. And as you (I assume) want to get yourself an author website, you bought this book. Well done you, excellent choice.

But what if you didn't want to buy a book? What if you don't have the available funds right now, or you need the information more quickly, or you want advice on something more specific than the topic of an entire book?

That's where the author's blog comes in.

Someone searching for information on the topic you write about may well come across a blog post from your website. They'll click through and read that. If it's useful and well-written, they'll browse your site looking for more (which is where having related posts at the bottom of each post comes in: see Chapter 7).

Having read their fill of your wonderful content, they'll then sign up to your mailing list. Or they might decide they need more detail and buy your book.

Hurray! You gained a fan, or made a sale. And without spending a penny on advertising.

I'm not denying that this is hard work. Keeping your blog buoyant in the search rankings means keeping it fresh and up to date, which means posting at least once a week.

But it can reap big rewards. Even more so if you're planning (or have already written) multiple books around related topics. People who follow your blog will be your audience for more than just the one book.

So what can you write about on your blog?

For a nonfiction author, I'm assuming this is an easier question. Things you could post to your blog include:

- Excerpts from your book(s).
- Quick tips telling people how to do something that's covered in your books.

- Tutorials—more in-depth posts with instructions.
- Opinion pieces. Don't shy away from expressing an opinion on your subject matter—it makes you stand out.
- Case studies. Tell readers about projects you've worked on or about your own progress. For example I have a series of posts on my blog that are all about my own experience taking my books wide, i.e. taking them out of Kindle Unlimited (wp4writers.com/wide).
- Interviews with other people working in your field. If you can bag an interview with someone who has a strong following, even better (I publish an interview with a fellow author on my blog every Friday: wp4writers.com/interviews.)
- Book reviews and recommendations—talking about books on topics related to yours won't eat into your own sales, it'll just make your blog a more useful resource.
- Video updates—show your visitors what you're up to and make videos of the projects you're working on or events you attend.

I'm sure you can think of plenty more that's relevant to your subject matter, but hopefully this has given you some inspiration.

The takeaway is: get blogging!

YOUR WEBSITE IS A POWERFUL (AND FREE) CONTENT MARKETING TOOL

I hope I've convinced you of the benefits of content marketing.

Content marketing is a long-term marketing activity. It won't get you quick sales in the way that paid advertising can (although learning how to run profitable ads is also a long game).

But it's free. And it makes use of a skill you already have: writing. You will need to adapt your writing style to the form of the blog post, as it's different from writing a novel or nonfiction book.

But if you see content marketing as a long-term strategy, especially if it's something you enjoy, it can reap big rewards. Reach out to new readers; build an army of fans; sell books.

Next, we're going to take a look at how this works in practice. Content marketing is all very well, but how do you actually do it on your WordPress site?

Never fear. This is what WordPress was made for.

18

WORDPRESS CONTENT TYPES: POSTS, PAGES AND MORE

WORDPRESS WAS ORIGINALLY DESIGNED as a blogging platform. Over the years, it's developed into a content management system (CMS), with extra features that'll let you get more from your site.

But at heart, it's still great for blogging.

In the following chapters, we're going to start working properly on content. I'll clarify what types of content you have available to you with WordPress and show you how to create it.

I'll also show you some ninja tricks: how to do more than just write and publish blog posts.

AN OVERVIEW OF CONTENT TYPES IN WORDPRESS

WordPress gives you two main content types: posts and pages.

Posts are your updates: news items, stories, musings, anything you want to share. This is the stuff that will be shared to your social media accounts and that people will receive in their inbox if they subscribe to your site.

Pages are different. They're constants of your site, pages which are designed to be easily accessed and to give people core information about you and your writing. They'll include things like your 'about me' page, your contact page and your landing page for email signups. Pages go in your navigation menu, while posts don't.

As well as posts and pages, you also have access to some other content types: media and comments. Let's take a look at each of these.

POSTS

Posts will be familiar to anyone who's ever run a blog. If you aren't familiar with blogging, you'll have read posts on news sites.

You'll be creating posts regularly, designed to keep your readers up to date with you and your writing.

As I've already mentioned, posts don't go in your navigation menu. Instead, you use categories to group your posts together, and then put those categories in your navigation menu.

So in my own website (rachelmcwrites.com), there are four main categories: websites, writing, productivity and publishing. All of these are in the main navigation menu at the top of the page, along with links to the static pages.

If you click on one of these, you're taken to something called an archive page: in this case a category archive. An archive page lists all of the posts in that category. You can also have archives for tags (more of which in the next chapter), and the main blog page is an archive of all your posts.

PAGES

A page is a piece of static content. It might be information about you and your writing, or the page with newsletter signups, or a page with information about your books and/or your story worlds.

Pages are designed to be evergreen: they're content that people will want to read regardless of when they first visit your site. This is different from posts, where people are more likely to read the most recent ones.

Most of the pages in your site will be in the navigation menu. There will be some exceptions to this: for example you need a privacy page if you're collecting email addresses, but shouldn't include it in your main navigation menu as it's not of much interest.

Instead, purely administrative pages can have a link in the footer or sidebar. You can add this using the ninja trick in Chapter 21.

MEDIA

You can add all sorts of media to your WordPress site: images, video, pdf files, audio, even spreadsheets if you want. The ones you'll be adding the most often will probably be images.

You can add media via the Media section of the admin screens or by uploading it directly to a page or post. You can also embed media such as video, which will save storage space in your site and be more reliable. You'll learn all about media in Chapter 23.

COMMENTS

And finally, we have comments. If you're like me and you live in terror of the trolls 'below the line', don't worry.

People don't generally come to writers' sites to cause trouble. It's not as if they're going to get a lot of attention. And if someone does make a comment that's offensive or inappropriate—well, it's your site. You can delete it.

Comments can be a powerful way of increasing engagement with and between your fans. At first your posts won't get many comments, but over time this will grow as your audience grows. You know you've really made it when your fans start talking to each other in the comments, and you don't have to get involved. Just sit back and let the fandom feed itself (while you get on with writing the next book).

WordPress gives you a number of tools for managing comments, which I'll cover in Chapter 32.

But first, we'll continue with content. Specifically, how you migrate content from another website.

If this isn't your first site, and you have posts and pages you want to move into your shiny new WordPress site, the next chapter is for you.

But if this is your first author website, then save yourself some work. Skip the next chapter and learn more about creating content with WordPress's new content creation feature: blocks.

19

SWITCHING FROM ANOTHER PLATFORM? HERE'S HOW TO MIGRATE YOUR CONTENT

BEFORE YOU START ADDING lots of shiny new content to your WordPress site, we're going to take a little detour. Imagine me turning the steering wheel and guiding you down a narrow country lane, one that will make your passage along the highway all that much smoother when you come back to it.

(OK, bad metaphor. I'll stop now.)

If you had another website before this one, and you're switching from that to your new WordPress site, you probably won't want to lose your content. Wouldn't it be great if there was a way to automatically copy everything over, which took no more than a few minutes?

Rejoice, dear friend, for I have the answer. And that's the WordPress Importer tool.

This will let you import content from another WordPress site or from another platform.

Of course, if this is your first author website and you don't need to migrate, you can have a pass. Flip to the next chapter and start creating some content.

WEBSITE PLATFORMS YOU CAN MIGRATE CONTENT FROM

At the time of writing, these are the platforms that you can migrate your content from and into WordPress:

- Blogger.
- Blogroll.
- LiveJournal.
- Medium.
- Movable Type.
- TypePad.
- Tumblr.
- Wix.
- Another WordPress site.

I don't know about you, but I haven't even heard of some of those platforms. LiveJournal, anyone? So I'm going to focus here on the most popular ones.

Some of these have plugins for WordPress.org that make it super easy to migrate, or an import tool in WordPress.com. Others let you export content via RSS and then import it using the RSS importer for WordPress.org.

That sounds horribly confusing, I know. So I'll give you an overview of how it works for each of the main platforms.

MIGRATING FROM BLOGGER

Here are the steps to importing your content from Blogger:

1. Open your Blogger site and log in.
2. Go to **Settings > Other** and click **Back up Content > Save to your computer**. This downloads an XML file with all your blog's content.
3. In WordPress.com, click on **Import** in the admin menu.

You'll see Blogger listed. Click on the **Start Import** button next to it.

4. In WordPress.org, go to **Tools > Import**. Under **Blogger**, click **Install Now** and once that's installed, click **Run Importer**.
5. In the next screen, upload the XML file from your computer that you downloaded in Step 2.
6. Click on **Start Import** or **Continue**. (Which you see will depend on whether you're using WordPress.com or WordPress.org.)
7. The system will ask you who the author of the posts you're importing should be: choose your own user account. It will then import your content, including images.
8. Check your posts and pages, as well as your images. If there are any problems, see the section on *Checking and Tweaking Your Content* below.

MIGRATING FROM MEDIUM

Importing from Medium to WordPress.org is tricky, and can only be done via a third-party tool. If you need to do this, check out wp4writers.com/medium or try the ninja trick later in this chapter.

But for some reason that I can't fathom, WordPress.com has an importer tool for Medium. Here are the steps to migrate your content:

1. Open Medium and log in.
2. Go to **Download your information**, and select **Download .zip**. You should receive an email from Medium with an export of your posts in a zip file.
3. In WordPress.com, go to **Import**. Next to **Medium**, click **Start import**.

4. Upload the zip file you received in your email and click **Continue**.
5. The system will import all of your content and you'll get an email when it's done.

MIGRATING FROM TUMBLR

If you had a Tumblr blog before, you can import all of your content to WordPress.com or WordPress.org. But the process is different for the two. Let's look at WordPress.com first, which makes it simpler.

MIGRATING FROM TUMBLR TO WORDPRESS.COM

1. Open WordPress.com and click **Import** in the admin menu.
2. Scroll to the bottom of the page and click **Other importers**.
3. A new screen will open with a list of more importers. Click on **Run importer** under **Tumblr**.
4. You'll be asked to sign into your Tumblr account to authenticate. Click **Connect to Tumblr** to begin and follow the instructions.
5. Sign into your Tumblr account and click **Allow** to allow the export.
6. You'll see a list of your Tumblr blogs. Select the ones you want to migrate by clicking **Import this blog**.
7. Your content will be imported and you'll get an email when it's done.

Note: Importing from Tumblr doesn't always run 100% smoothly. For more information on migrating from Tumblr to WordPress.com, see wp4writers.com/tumblr.

MIGRATING FROM TUMBLR TO WORDPRESS.ORG

Migrating between Tumblr and a self-hosted WordPress site is more complicated. To do it, you'll need to create an app in Tumblr.

Note: If you don't relish the thought of doing all this, try the ninja trick later in this chapter.

1. In WordPress, go to **Tools > Import**. Under **Tumblr**, click **Install Now** and once that's installed, click **Run Importer**.
2. The next screen will give you instructions for creating an app. Follow those instructions.
3. Type in your OAuth consumer key and your secret key. Click on **Connect to Tumblr**.
4. Sign into your Tumblr account and click **Allow** to allow the export.
5. You'll see a list of your Tumblr blogs. Select the ones you want to migrate by clicking **Import this blog**.
6. Your content will be imported and you'll get a notification when it's done.
7. Check your posts and pages, as well as your images. If there are any problems, see the section on *Checking and Tweaking Your Content* below.

For a step-by-step tutorial on migrating from Tumblr to Word-Press.org, go to wp4writers.com/tumblr2.

MIGRATING FROM WIX

Again, importing from Wix is different depending on whether you're on WordPress.com or WordPress.org. Let's start with Word-Press.com.

MIGRATING FROM WIX TO WORDPRESS.COM

1. In WordPress.com, click **Import** in the admin menu.
2. Next to **Wix**, click **Start import**.
3. Type in the URL of your existing site and click **Continue**.
4. WordPress will import your content.

Now that couldn't be any simpler, could it? You don't even have to log in to Wix (not sure how I feel about the plagiarism implications there, but let's just put a pin in that issue).

MIGRATING FROM WIX TO WORDPRESS.ORG

Importing from Wix to WordPress.org is, you guessed it, a bit more complicated. Follow the steps below or try the ninja trick later in this chapter.

This method involves getting the RSS feed from your Wix site. It's the RSS feed that WordPress.com uses, which is why it's so easy.

1. Go to your Wix site and add an RSS button to your site following the instructions at wp4writers.com/wixrss (don't get me started on why this is the only way to get the RSS feed for a Wix site, it should be so much easier).
2. Now visit your Wix site and click on the RSS button.
3. Right-click anywhere on the page with the feed (it should be an unintelligible page of code). Click **Save as** and save the file to your computer.
4. Now in WordPress, click on **Tools > Import**.
5. Under RSS, click **Install Now** and then **Run Importer**.
6. Upload the file you just saved to your computer from Wix. Click **Upload file and import**.
7. WordPress will upload and import your posts.

Note: This method of importing doesn't import any images and it's unreliable when it comes to pages. You'll need to clean things up or use the ninja trick described later. (Have I got you begging for this ninja trick yet?)

MIGRATING FROM WORDPRESS

Now for the easy one. Migrating between two WordPress sites is easy and reliable, as you might expect. You can migrate between WordPress.com or WordPress.org sites or from one platform to the other.

Let's start with migrating into WordPress.com. First, I'll work through exporting your content from one WordPress.com site, then importing into another one. If you're migrating from WordPress.com to WordPress.org, follow the first step here and then the second step for WordPress.org. Or vice versa!

EXPORTING FROM WORDPRESS.COM

First you need to export your content into a file. It's not as hard as that makes it sound, I promise!

1. In WordPress.com, go to **Settings** from the admin menu. Scroll down to the **Site Tools** section. Click on **Export**.
2. On the next screen, click on **Export all**.
3. WordPress will create an export file and email you with a link to download it.

IMPORTING TO WORDPRESS.COM

Follow these steps if you're migrating from one WordPress.com site to another or from self-hosted WordPress to WordPress.com (not something many people do, but you never know…)

1. In WordPress.com, click **Import** in the admin menu.
2. Next to WordPress, click on the **Start Import** button.
3. In the next screen, upload the file you downloaded from your old WordPress site.
4. Click **Continue**.
5. WordPress will prompt you to check which user account to assign posts to and to check you want to import media (you do).
6. WordPress will import all of your content.

EXPORTING FROM WORDPRESS.ORG

Now let's switch to WordPress.org. Here's what you need to do if you want to export a WordPress.org site so you can import your content to another WordPress.org site or to WordPress.com.

1. In WordPress, go to **Tools > Export**.
2. Under Choose what to export, select **All content**.
3. Click the **Download Export File** button.
4. WordPress will create an export file and download it to your computer.

IMPORTING TO WORDPRESS.ORG

Now let's see how you can import content from WordPress.com or WordPress.org into your new WordPress.org site.

1. In WordPress, go to **Tools > Import**.
2. Under **WordPress**, click **Install Now** and then **Run Importer**.
3. WordPress will ask you to find the export file you downloaded after exporting from your old WordPress site. Don't worry if this is from WordPress.com or WordPress.org—they work in the same way.
4. Find the file and click the **Upload file and import** button.

5. WordPress will ask you which user account you want to associate the new content with—it'll normally be your own account. It will also ask you to verify that you want to import media. You do.

6. Wait while WordPress imports the new content, then go to the Posts section of your site. You'll find it full of your content.

NINJA TRICK

And that's how you migrate your old site into WordPress.

But some of those methods for importing into WordPress.org were pretty horrible. Add RSS buttons, creating apps? You don't want to do that.

For some of the examples above, importing into WordPress.com is way easier than importing into WordPress.org.

So here's my ninja trick to make the process easier. It involves importing and exporting content twice, but will rely on WordPress to do the work for you, so you don't have to do anything tricky like creating apps or finding RSS feeds.

1. Create an account at WordPress.com. I recommend doing this anyway if you've got a self-hosted WordPress site, so that you can use the Jetpack plugin (see Chapter 16). If you've already installed Jetpack, just log into the WordPress.com account you set up then, and create a new site.

2. Create a free site on WordPress.com. Don't bother changing the theme, adding plugins, or tweaking the site settings.

3. Import your content from your old site to your new WordPress.com site, using the relevant method detailed above.

4. Check your posts in WordPress.com. Have all of the

images migrated over? If not, you can either upload them manually now or wait until you're in your WordPress.org site (which I'd recommend).

5. Now export your content from your new WordPress.com site using the method I outlined in the WordPress section above. Save the file to your computer.

6. Import your content from your WordPress.com site to your WordPress.org site.

7. In WordPress.org, check that everything's copied across correctly. See the section below on checking and tweaking your content.

8. Back in WordPress.com, open your dummy site. You don't want this site anymore, so it's time to delete it. Go to **Settings** in the admin menu. Scroll down to the bottom of the screen and click **Delete your site permanently**. WordPress will ask you to confirm that you want to do this; go through the process to delete your site.

You'll now have a new site in WordPress.org with the content from your old site in Wix, Medium or Tumblr, and a Word-Press.com account which will be associated with this site if you've already installed Jetpack or will have no site associated with it if you haven't. If you want to use the WordPress.com features via the Jetpack plugin, go to Chapter 16 for instructions.

CHECKING AND TWEAKING YOUR CONTENT

Phew!

Depending on the platform you were migrating from, you've either just followed a simple process that took a few minutes, or you've spent half an hour working through it.

Either way, this is much quicker and easier than manually creating all of the content from your old site again.

But you're not done yet.

It's time to check all of your posts, and in particular your media, and ensure it copied across correctly.

If you migrated between two WordPress sites, the chances are things migrated across very smoothly. But with the other platforms, there may be a few glitches.

Check all of the posts and check that the images are displaying. You may find that some images have migrated across to your media library in your new site, but aren't showing up on the right post.

If this is the case, you'll need to edit the post:

1. Open the post in the admin (click on **Edit post** in the admin bar while you're viewing it on the live site or find it in the Posts screen).
2. Find the spot in the post where you want the image to appear.
3. Hover over the block below it (which will be a paragraph or another image) and click on the **+** icon at the top of the block. (*Note: if you aren't seeing blocks, it means you're migrating from an older version of WordPress that didn't use blocks. Click on where it says* **Classic** *at the top of the post, click the three dots at the right-hand side of the menu that appears, and click the* **Convert to blocks** *option. There's more on blocks in the next chapter.*)
4. Select **Image**.
5. Click the **Media Library** button and search for your image in the media library. If it's not there, upload it instead.
6. Insert the image into the text.

There's more on blocks in Chapter 20 and on working with images and other media in Chapter 23.

Congratulations! You now have a new WordPress site with all of the content from your old site. I think you've earned a coffee. Go and make one while you plan all that lovely content you're going to create.

Then it's time to add some new content.

CREATING CONTENT WITH BLOCKS

I THOUGHT LONG and hard about this section of the book.

In fact, I kept moving it around.

Blocks are new to WordPress. They're designed to give you something closer to the drag-and-drop interface you get with website builders like Wix, and over time I believe they will evolve and change.

So I don't want to spend too much time on them, in case what I write is out of date by the time you read this.

But without understanding blocks, it's very hard for you to create content in WordPress.

I think blocks are pretty nifty. They make it easier for you to move content around than it used to be, they provide lots of extra content types you can add to your posts and pages, and they let you create reusable content you can use time and time again on different parts of your site.

They will change and evolve, but I'd be a real meanie if I didn't tell you more about them. So I'm going to give you an introduction to blocks and an overview of how to use them.

In this section, I'm going to assume you've created at least one post or page, and you're working with that. Don't worry about how literary or erudite the content is: you can always create a post just to play around with and test ideas on, and them keep it as a draft or delete it if you want.

So before you start working with those blocks, you'll need to either go to the editing screen for your post or page, or create one. If you need to know how to do this, see Chapter 5 for Word-Press.com or Chapter 12 for WordPress.org.

CREATING CONTENT WITH BLOCKS

Now it's time to create some content in your page. At last!

To start adding text, just start typing. Every time you hit Return on your keyboard, WordPress will create a new block. Each block contains one element: a paragraph, a list, an image, or something else.

I'm not going to devote too much space in this book to blocks, precisely because they're so new. Chances are they'll change quite quickly: there'll be more options added, the ones that are already there will change, and some of them might disappear.

But for now, here are the block types you're most likely to use:

- Text blocks: paragraph, list, quote, verse.
- Media blocks: image, gallery, file, video.
- Formatting blocks: table, custom HTML.
- Layout elements: button, columns, separator.
- Widgets: shortcode, latest posts, latest comments, categories.
- Embeds: social media feeds, video.

That's not an exhaustive list of the blocks available to you, but it does include the ones I think you're most likely to need. If you want to add blocks, click on the **+** sign at the top of an existing block and you'll see a list of all the blocks available. Alternatively you can click the **+** sign at the top left of the screen.

And if you install a plugin with blocks, you'll get more blocks from that plugin. So if you install a plugin to link to your mailing list, for example, you might find that it gives you a block to add a mailing list signup form. Neat!

Spend some time adding content to your page. To add paragraphs, just type away. If you want to convert existing paragraphs to a list, select the text, click on the button with the arrows to the top left of the text, and select **List**.

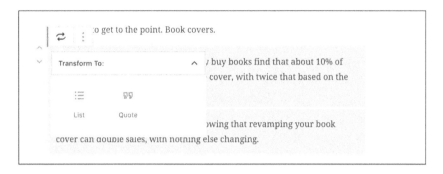

Image 20-1 Transform paragraph to list

You can also add media items by clicking the **+** sign to add a new block, selecting the media type you want and then uploading your media. My recommendation for media is to upload images to your site but embed video instead. You'll find out more about media of all types in Chapter 23.

NINJA TRICK: SHORTCUT MENU

A quick way to create a new block type is to hit the Return key after your paragraph as if creating a new paragraph block, then hit the slash (/) key. This will pull up a shortcut menu with the most commonly used blocks for you to choose from. Nifty!

EDITING BLOCKS

Once you've created a block, you can edit it. You can change its block type and edit the content. Let's take a look at some of the options.

CHANGING THE BLOCK TYPE

You can only change the block type to another similar block type. So for example you can change a paragraph block to a list block or an image block to a gallery block. But you can't turn a gallery block into a paragraph block. To do that, you'd have to delete the bock then create a new one from scratch.

To change the block type, click on the block and a context-specific mini-menu will appear above it. The item on the left-hand side will be an icon representing the type of block it is. Click on that and you'll see a **Transform to:** menu. Select the type of block you'd like to change it to.

I find this particularly useful for lists: I'll just type the items in the list, hitting the **Return** key after each line, then select all the paragraphs and turn them into a list. You can do this with multiple blocks at once.

EDITING TEXT BLOCKS

You can also edit the content of your block using that mini-menu that appears above it when you click on it. The items in your menu will depend on the block type, so with text blocks you'll find text editing options.

And you can edit blocks from the Block pane on the right-hand side of the screen.

For text blocks, you can change things like the color and text size: but I'd strongly advise you not to. If you start messing with the colors in your text, it will clash with the styling in your theme (or any changes you made via the Customizer), and will make your site look messy and unprofessional. Just trust your theme to look after the visual design for you.

ADDING LINKS

Something else I find myself doing a lot is adding links to the text. To do this, you click on the block, select the text you want to use as a link, then click the link icon in the mini-menu above. You'll be presented with a field where you type in the URL that you want the link to point to. It's much better to use existing text within your content for links than it is to just type the link into the text.

CREATING HEADINGS

Another thing you can do with text blocks is turn them into headings. Click on the block, and then the paragraph icon, and select **Transform to: > Heading**. You'll be given the option of different levels of heading: **H2**, **H3** etc.

It's important to use a logical, hierarchical structure for your headings, as this helps with your site's SEO and accessibility. Your theme will put the title of the page or post in a H1 tag, so any subheadings you add within the text should be at the H2 level. If you add further subheadings under those (in other words, in a hierarchical structure of headings), use H3. I rarely have cause to use H4—if you do, your post is probably too long and complicated! Try splitting it into two shorter posts and giving your readers twice as much to look at and search engines twice as many opportunities to find your site.

Other text options are block quotes, preformatted (used for code: probably not much use to most people reading this book), and verse: useful if you're a poet.

NINJA TRICK: REUSABLE BLOCKS

One of my favorite features of blocks is something called reusable blocks.

These let you create a block once, save it, and then add it to other posts or pages in your site without having to start again. If you edit any examples of the block, all of them will update.

This is really useful for text you want to include in all of your posts, such as an encouragement to sign up to your mailing list.

To create a reusable block, start by creating a block in one of your posts in the usual way. Make sure it's working exactly as you want it to. Then click on the block and select the ellipsis (three dots one above the other) on the right of the mini-menu. Select **Add to Reusable Blocks**. You'll see a field where you type in the name of your reusable block: give it a memorable name and click the **Save** button.

Now save your post and create a new one. To add the reusable block to it, click the **+** icon to create a new block, then select **Reusable** from the block types given. You will see a list of all your reusable blocks.

Select the reusable block you want to use, and it will appear in your post. Nice!

I like to create a post with all of my reusable blocks in it and then keep that post as a draft, never publishing it. That way, I have one place to go if I want to edit my reusable blocks or add to them in the future.

WordPress will automatically save your post as a draft until you publish it. Find out more about drafts in Chapter 22.

Blocks are the tools you use to create the content of your posts and pages. But what on earth do you write in them?

Let's start by looking at pages, and how you might use them.

TELL THE WORLD ABOUT YOURSELF WITH PAGES

So, you now have one of three things:

- An empty site ready for you to add lots of shiny new content to it.
- A site with all of the content from your old site migrated into it.
- A massive headache and a longing to get back to writing instead of working on your website.

OK, so I'm hoping you don't have the third. But if it is, give yourself a break. You've done the tricky stuff and if you've migrated your site from Tumblr to self-hosted WordPress, you've earned yourself a medal. Give up writing right now and get yourself a lucrative career as a geek.

In this chapter, I'm going to show you how to create pages in your site. If you remember from earlier on, these are static pages that you create once and that are designed to be (relatively) evergreen. Things like your 'About me' page and your 'Books' page.

A NOTE ON THE HOME PAGE

The home page can be a little confusing. Is it a page, or is it a list of posts?

Well, it can be either. Here are the two options WordPress gives you:

1. A STATIC HOME PAGE

Your home page is a static page, with content that you write to go on that page. It'll welcome people to the site and give them an idea of what to expect.

I use a static page for all of my websites, because I like to say hi to people when they land on my site and give them some useful links that will help them find their way around. This is because reading my latest blog post might not be the best option for everyone who visits.

Image 21-1 The home page of the RachelMcWrites website

If you go for the static home page option, you'll also need a page to hold your blog posts. To do this, you create an empty page called 'Blog' and then tell WordPress to use that for your posts. Once you've done that, WordPress won't let you add any content to that page yourself, as it's all done automatically.

Having a static home page doesn't mean you can't have your blog posts listed on the home page as well—I always add a widget to my sidebar with my latest posts, so people can access them from anywhere in the site. Or alternatively, you can add a Widget block to your home page with the latest posts in it. (For detailed instructions on this, go to wp4writers.com/homepage.)

If you're a fiction author, people will come to your site wanting to know more about you and your books. I'd recommend a static home page. But if you're a nonfiction author, your blog might be the most important thing on your site, in which case, you might prefer your posts on your home page...

2. POSTS ON THE HOME PAGE

The second option is for your home page to be an archive of your latest posts. It'll display the ten most recent posts, and you can choose whether visitors will see an excerpt of each post or the full post.

I prefer excerpts, since scrolling through ten posts can take a very long time. Excerpts can also look very effective if your theme displays them next to the featured image for the post, which is a special image designed to represent the post.

Image 21-2 The RachelMcWrites blog page

If your site is focused on your blog, then it makes sense to put your blog posts on the home page. If you do go with that option, you don't need to create a page for your home page or your blog posts: WordPress will automatically generate a home page for you with your blog posts listed.

Once you've decided what kind of home page you want, you need to tell WordPress what you've chosen, By default, posts on your home page will be selected. If you want to switch to a static home page, you'll need to create two pages ('Home' and 'Blog'), and then go to **Settings > Reading** to configure things.

If you're on WordPress.com, this is covered in Chapter 5, and for WordPress.org, it's in Chapter 12.

HOW TO CREATE A PAGE

You've probably already created a couple of quick pages for testing with your content. But if you haven't, or if you've forgotten how, here's the skinny:

- In WordPress.org, go to **Site Pages > Add**.
- In WordPress.com, go to **Pages > Add New**.

You'll see the page editing screen where you can start creating your content.

Why is this different in WordPress.com and WordPress.org?

As you work through this section of the site, you'll see multiple instances of the WordPress.com and WordPress.org interfaces being very slightly different. This is because they're built on the same software (the software you downloaded if you installed WordPress manually on your hosting), but WordPress.com has some tweaks to make it (supposedly) more user-friendly.

Over time, it's likely that WordPress.org will have the same menu items as WordPress.com, so if what you see isn't exactly the same as what's on the screen, it's because there's been an update.

USING PAGE TEMPLATES (IF YOUR THEME HAS THEM)

Some themes come with a feature called page templates. This means that there's more than one possible layout for your pages.

The most common alternative page template is a full-width template. This displays the page content across the full width of the page, with no sidebar. If you have a static home page, you might want to use this template to increase the visual impact of your page: it's what I do for my fiction site.

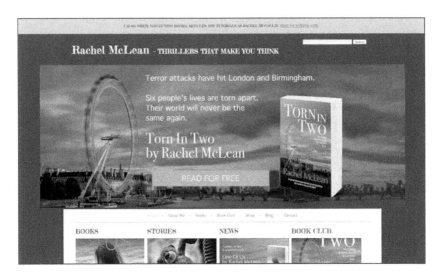

Image 21-3 The Rachel McLean website

Each theme will have a default template, which will be the one used if you don't select a different one. This is normally the template with a sidebar.

To change the template for your page, open up the page editing screen for it and make sure the admin bar on the right-hand side is on the **Document** tab and not the **Block** tab. Scroll down to the **Page Attributes** section and click the downwards arrow to open it up.

If your theme does have multiple templates, you'll see a drop-down list called **Template**. Select the template you want to use from the list. You can preview how it looks before saving your changes by clicking the **Preview** button at the top left of the screen.

Image 21-4 Page templates

Note: If you can't see this dropdown list, it means your theme only has one page template. Sorry!

STRUCTURING PAGES

WordPress also lets you structure the pages in your site into a hierarchical, or tree-like structure.

So if you have a page for each of your book series for example, you can place all of these under your main Books page.

First you create the top-level page, or parent page in WordPress terminology. This can be your Books page. Then create a page for your series, and give that a parent page. Go to the **Page Attributes** section in the **Document** tab again, and select the **Parent Page** dropdown list. Find the **Books** page and select it.

Once you've done this, the hierarchy will be shown in your main **Pages** screen. Here's an example from one of my websites. In this case, I have a section for my story worlds, with a page for each of the locations.

Worlds	Rachel McCollin	—	—	ııl	—	✎ No title
— San Francisco	Rachel McCollin	—	Murder in the Multiverse	ııl	—	✎ No title
— Silicon City	Rachel McCollin	—	Murder in the Multiverse	ııl	—	✎ No title
— Fogtown	Rachel McCollin	—	—	ııl	—	✎ No title
— Greater Castro	Rachel McCollin	—	—	ııl	—	✎ No title
— New Paris	Rachel McCollin	—	—	ııl	—	✎ No title
— Point Zero	Rachel McCollin	—	—	ııl	—	✎ No title
Your FREE story	Rachel McCollin	—	—	ııl	—	✎ No title

Image 21-5 Pages in a hierarchy

Note: The Pages screen looks a bit different on WordPress.com and WordPress.org, but gives you the same information.

HELPING PEOPLE FIND YOUR PAGE VIA THE NAVIGATION MENU

Once you've created your pages, you want people to find them.

As they won't show up in your blog page or any archives (because they're static content, not posts), you need to add them to the navigation menu.

Navigation menus for WordPress.com are covered in detail in Chapter 6 and for WordPress.org in Chapter 13, but here's a recap of how you add a page to the menu.

In WordPress.com, go to **Customize** and click **Menus**. In WordPress.org, you can either use the Customizer or go to **Appearance > Menus**.

Select the menu to which you want to add your page (your main navigation menu). If you only have one menu on your site, it will already be selected.

Find your page from the pages listed and add it to the menu. You can edit the text that's used to link to the page. So if you have a page called 'About Me', you might prefer to call the link *About*.

Finally, save your menu (in the Customizer, click **Publish**, in the Menus screen, click **Save Menu**).

If you visit your site, you'll now find that your page has been added to the navigation menu.

Ninja Trick: Adding a Page to a Custom Menu

If you've got pages in your site that you don't want to add to the main menu but you do want people to be able to access (e.g. your privacy page), you can create an extra menu in the Customizer or the Menus screen with that page.

Once you've done that, you can add the Custom Menu widget to your sidebar or footer and that menu will be displayed.

I like to add these to my footer to give people access to pages not in the main navigation menu. For example, you could create a menu for all of your series, and add just the main Books page to the navigation menu.

HELP! MY PAGE HAS A GLARING TYPO!

So you've created your page and published it, gone to your site to take a look at it and—yikes!—there's an error.

Never fear. Editing pages is really easy.

If you're logged in to your WordPress site, you can click **Edit Page** in the admin bar at the top of the screen when you're viewing it, and you'll be taken straight to the editing screen for the page. If you aren't logged in, you'll need to log in and then access the page via the main **Pages** screen. (I like to log in, then use the back button in my browser to go back to the live page, refresh it and then use the link in the admin bar.)

Just amend whatever you need to, then click the **Update** button at the top right of the editing screen. This will be where the **Publish** button was when you were originally creating the page.

Of course this isn't just for fixing errors: you can edit the page to update information in it at any point, or change the images in it, for example.

Once you've done that, your changes will be published and no one will be any the wiser about your typo.

DELETING PAGES

Sometimes you decide you don't like a page anymore. Perhaps it said something to offend you. Perhaps it's full of dreadful prose. Or perhaps you just created it by mistake or for testing.

You have three options when it comes to deleting pages:

- You can set them to draft so people can't see them.
- You can move them to the trash.
- You can permanently delete them.

To make a page into a draft (meaning you can come back and edit it sometime if you'd like), open the page editing screen and click the **Switch to Draft** link at the top right of the screen. This will change the page's status to draft, meaning no one can see it but you.

To trash a page, click the **Move to Trash** button in the **Document** tab on the right hand side of the page editing screen.

To permanently delete a page, you'll have to go to the Trash screen and delete it (you can only delete pages you've already put in the trash). Go to the main Pages screen and click on the **Trash** tab at the top. You'll see all the pages in the trash. From here you can either restore the page or delete it. In WordPress.com, click on the ellipsis to the far right of the page name to see a menu with those two options and click the one you want. In WordPress.org, hover your mouse over the page name and click the **Restore** or **Delete Permanently** link beneath it.

Once you've deleted a page permanently, there's no way to get it back (other than resorting your site from a backup). So it's wise to just leave pages you don't want in the trash.

In WordPress.org, you can also move published or draft pages to the trash by hovering over them in the Pages screen and clicking the **Trash** link in the list below.

So that's pages. Once you've created a few, they won't be something you spend too much time with.

No, the content you'll be adding the most frequently is posts. Read on for tips on using them in your author blog.

22

KEEP YOUR FANS UPDATED WITH POSTS

ASSUMING you've decided you're going to keep your site's content regularly updated, the thing you'll spend the most time doing is creating posts.

These are designed to provide a time-sensitive update on what you're up to, and will be displayed on your main blog page as well as on category archive pages.

So let's dive into creating and editing posts.

BEFORE YOU START: TIDYING UP

Before you start adding new content, it's wise to tidy up those dummy posts you added for testing with your theme.

You can either edit these to make them into 'proper' posts, or you can delete them.

You can trash or delete posts, or convert them to drafts, in exactly the same way as you do pages. So instead of repeating that here, I'm going to point you in the direction of the previous chapter, where that's explained in detail.

YES, YOU'RE A BLOGGER: CREATE YOUR FIRST POST

If you've read the chapter on content marketing, then you should have some awesome ideas for what you can include in your posts. If you don't have lots of ideas yet, don't worry: the ideas will come. For example, I received a question on Facebook recently asking me for advice on choosing hosting for an author website. I answered the question and have used it as the basis for a blog post. Ideas will come from all sorts of sources.

Writing your first post can feel daunting, and seeing it sitting alone on the Blog page can feel a little sad. So it's a good idea when you first start, to write three or more posts and publish them all together. They don't all have to be given the same date—you can assign a date in the past to a post, just as you can schedule it for the future (more of which shortly).

When you create a new post, you'll be faced with an empty screen. Just start typing, and WordPress will automatically create blocks for you. These will be paragraphs, lists, images and more.

You can find out all about blocks in Chapter 20 and media in Chapter 23.

WRITING A GREAT BLOG POST

This book isn't a guide to blogging or to copywriting, but I think it's worth including some tips on writing blog posts, as they are different from writing novels or even nonfiction books.

The important thing is to keep your writing engaging and enticing. Copywriting (of which blogging is an example) has its own set of skills and techniques, but here's the tip I find most useful:

Each sentence is designed to get the reader to read the next sentence.

That's it. Pretty simple, huh? Your copy should pull people along, being entertaining, informative, or maybe (hallelujah!) both. Don't try to create gorgeous literary tracts: this is a quick-consumption medium that's designed to engage people and encourage them to read more.

The first sentence will lead them to read the second sentence...

Which will lead them to read the third sentence...

And so on until they reach the end of the post...

Where you'll have links encouraging them to read more posts...

And a link to your newsletter signup page, so they can discover more about you and ultimately read your books.

Like I say, this is a long game. But a free and robust one.

Here are a few more tips on writing blog posts people will want to read:

- Avoid long paragraphs. Vary the length of sentences and paragraphs to keep things interesting.
- Make your first sentence a hook. A question, a bold statement, or a hint at something to come.
- Keep the tone light and fast-paced.
- Use the first and third persons. "My favorite book is *Moby Dick*, what's yours?" is much more engaging than, "*Moby Dick* is an excellent book, it would be interesting to know what readers think".
- Ask questions. Encourage people to add their thoughts or reactions in the comments.
- Use the Related Posts feature in WordPress.com or via the Jetpack plugin to add links to similar posts at the end of each blog post.
- Keep your blog posts to between 1,000 and 2,000 words. If you find yourself writing anything longer, split it into two posts. That gives you twice the Google juice and twice the opportunity to reach an audience.
- Talking of Google, don't artificially cram keywords into your posts. A well-written post by someone who knows their subject (that's you) will rank in the search engines. You don't need to force it.

This is by no means an exhaustive guide to copywriting. But the tips above might help you get started.

It pays to analyze the popularity of your posts. If you're on WordPress.com or you're using Jetpack (can you tell I'm a fan of Jetpack?), then you'll have access to a screen with stats for your site by year, month, week and day, and you'll also be able to see which posts are the most popular. If a post takes off, make sure you write more like it.

GIVING YOUR POST SOME CATEGORIES AND TAGS

Once you've written your post, it helps if you can categorize it. WordPress gives you two options for this:

- **Categories** are a bit like sections of your site. So on my site, for example, the categories are 'Websites & Newsletters', 'Writing & Plotting', 'Publishing & Marketing', and 'Productivity'. These are the sections of my site, that are in my navigation menu.
- **Tags** are designed to help people see lower-level links between content on your site. For example, the tags in my site include 'WordPress', 'MailChimp', 'landing pages', and 'self-publishing'. Some of these are subsets of the main categories, but most of them will cross category boundaries (if a tag can do something so grand without a passport).

Readers will access categories via a link to the archive page in the navigation menu. But you'll generate dozens of tags over time, and don't want to confuse people by adding them to navigation. The best way to give access to tags is via the Tag Cloud widget, which you can add to your sidebar or footer. I tend to add it to the footer as I prefer to highlight recent posts and a link to my news-letter signup in my sidebar.

WORKING WITH CATEGORIES

When you're editing a post, you can find categories and tags in the **Document** tab on the right. Scroll down to the **Categories** section and check the categories you want to assign to this post. You can use more than one category: so a hypothetical post on my blog about selling books via your website might be included in 'Websites & Newsletters' and also in 'Publishing & Marketing'.

If the category you want isn't there, or you haven't added any categories yet, click the **Add New Category** link and type in the name of the new category. Then when you save the post, that category will be made available to future posts (and existing ones if you edit them: time travel is indeed possible with WordPress).

Can I Create Categories Without Writing a New Post?

Excellent question. You can.

In the WordPress.org admin menu, go to **Posts > Categories**. In WordPress.com, go to **Settings > Writing** and click **Categories**.

This takes you to a screen where you can create and edit categories and see how many posts are already in your blog for each category.

Some people like to use this screen to create categories before they start adding any content. Whether you do this or you add them via the post editing screen is up to you.

WORKING WITH TAGS

Tags work in a similar way to categories, although you can't see them all listed when you're editing your post in the same way you do categories.

To assign tags to a post, open that **Document** tab on the right-hand side of the post editing screen, then find the **Tags** section (no surprise there). Start typing in the tag you want to use. WordPress will auto-complete the tag if there's already one set up with the same opening, or it will create a new one for you if you type in its name and hit the **Return** key.

You can add as many tags to a post as you like: hundreds if you're feeling like wasting your time.

You can also see the tags you've added to your site and edit them in the same way as you can with categories, via the Tags editing screen.

CATEGORIES AND TAGS ON THE LIVE SITE

So what? you're thinking. *It's all very well adding categories and tags, but what's the point?*

As your blog grows, and the number of posts increases, categories and tags will help your visitors find their way around. A Tag Cloud widget might help people who are looking for a very specific topic, and the category archives will help people identify sections of your site that are most relevant to them.

Many themes also display categories and tags at the end of each blog post. So there'll be a list of all the categories and tags that apply to this post.

Posted in Publishing & Marketing
Tagged Book marketing, cover design, genres |

Image 22-1 A list of categories and tags at the end of a post

This will encourage people to click through to find more posts in the same category and with the same tags. If they click on one of those links, they'll be taken to the archive for that category or tag, with every post in that category or tag listed. So if I click on the **Author interview** tag below my post, I get the tag archive.

Image 22-2 The tag archive

By default, the archive will have a heading with a list of the posts, most recent first. But what if I wanted to jazz up my category and tag archives by adding an introductory paragraph?

CREATING CATEGORY OR TAG DESCRIPTIONS

A category or tag description will add a paragraph or two or text at the top of the category or tag archive, telling visitors more about that category or tag.

To add a description, go to the Categories or Tags editing screen (**Posts > Categories** or **Posts > Tags** in WordPress.org, **Settings > Writing > Categories** or **Settings > Writing > Tags** in WordPress.com).

Select the category or tag you want to add a description for, type in the description, and save it. You'll now see that text at the top of your category or tag archive.

Image 22-3 The tag description on an archive page

Help! My description isn't showing up.

If the description doesn't appear on your archive page, that'll be the fault of your theme.

The theme needs to have some specific code in it for tag and category descriptions to be displayed, and a few themes don't include it.

The only options are to accept that, or to switch to a theme that does include it. Sorry!

SAVING AND PUBLISHING YOUR POST

When you're happy with your post, you can preview it and then publish it. Or if you're a rider at the gates of dawn who takes no prisoners, you can go ahead and publish it without previewing.

But WordPress doesn't like carefree types who publish posts

without stopping and checking (I know!), which is why you'll be given some publish checks before you finally set it to live.

Here's an overview of the publishing process that I recommend:

1. Write the post, add any media to it and check it for errors or typos. Save it as a draft. It's a good idea to leave your post for a few hours before coming back to edit it, so you have a clearer head.
2. Add a featured image if you have one. Many themes will use the featured image next to the post title on your main blog page and your archive pages. The image will be a clickable link through to your post. A featured image will also be used when your post is shared to social media, which will increase click rates. You'll find the featured image in the **Document** tab on the right.
3. Add an excerpt. Again, this is in the **Document** tab. If you don't add a manual except, WordPress will automatically use the first 55 characters of the post as an excerpt in archive pages, which isn't ideal. Adding a manual one means you can entice people to read the post.
4. Click the **Save Draft** link. Once you've done that, click the **Preview** button. This will open up a new tab in your browser with a preview of your post.
5. This is where you tend to find the glaring typo that you didn't spot in the editing screen. It's similar to the way you can find errors in a book when you edit a paper copy instead of the original manuscript on your computer: changing the context makes errors easier to spot.
6. Switch back to your post editing screen and make any changes you need to.
7. Add the title and description for search engines, using the fields provided by your SEO plugin (see Chapter 25).
8. Hit the **Publish** button.
9. WordPress will ask you if you're sure. If any of the suggestions given make you slap your forehead and curse

yourself for forgetting something important, go back and edit again.

10. If you are happy, hit **Publish** again.
11. Your post will appear live on your site. Congratulations! You're a blogger.

NINJA TRICKS

WordPress has some nifty tricks you can use to have even more control over your posts. Let's take a look at them.

SCHEDULING POSTS FOR THE FUTURE

You don't have to set your posts to publish at the time you actually publish them.

Instead, you can give a post a publication date in the past or in the future.

Using dates in the past is less common, although it's a good trick for when you're setting up your blog and adding your first posts. If you create three or four posts and give them dates in the past, it makes your blog look more established. Don't go nuts—you don't want people thinking you last posted in 1929—but instead, set one post for today, one for last week, and another for the week before.

That way, as soon as you publish those posts, it looks like you've got a blog that's been running for a few weeks. I won't tell.

But the really useful trick is scheduling posts: in other words, getting your post ready to publish, but giving it a publication date in the future.

If you do this, WordPress will automatically publish the post when the date you've set rolls around. So you can be sleeping (or working on your novel, or watching the Superbowl) when your post is published.

This gives you two benefits:

- You can write multiple posts at once and schedule them for the future, allowing you to manage your time better.
- You can publish posts at the time when you know your audience will be paying attention. This might be when you're asleep, or you're otherwise busy.

Scheduling Really Works

A while back, I was booked to speak at a conference.

I had a blog post lined up and ready to go that would support my talk. I wanted it to go live at the moment I sat down from speaking, and to share it on Twitter.

But I knew I'd be way too busy fighting off the hordes of admiring fans (OK, maybe going for a coffee with the person at the front who knew more about the topic than I did). So I wrote the post before leaving home, worked out when I'd be sitting down from my talk, scheduled the post to go live at that exact moment, and had the Jetpack plugin installed with social media auto-posting.

It worked. My tweet was liked and shared by people who'd been at the conference session and it prompted discussion of some of the ideas I raised. And it was all done in advance.

To schedule a post, open the **Document** tab on the right of the editing screen. Click on the **Immediately** link next to **Publish**. You'll be presented with a date picker. Use it to select the date and time when you want the post to go live.

You'll notice that the **Publish** button at the top of the screen becomes a **Schedule** button.

Now finish working on your post, do your pre-publication checks, and hit **Schedule** instead of **Publish**.

STICKY POSTS

Another nifty WordPress feature is sticky posts.

These are bit like pinned posts in Facebook or twitter. If you make a post sticky, it will always show up at the top of the main blog page or at the top of any archive page it appears in.

So if you've written a post that's really popular, or that highlights your literary genius in a way that your other posts don't quite manage, you can make it sticky and people will always be able to find it.

To make a post stick, go to the **Document** tab on the right (yes, we're in that tab again, it's where all the goodies are), and check the box where it says **Stick to the front page**.

Simple!

QUICK EDIT

Sometimes you finish a post, publish it, and then realize you need to change something. Maybe you want to make it sticky, or you forgot to add it to a category or two.

You could go back into the post editing screen and edit it again, but there is a shortcut.

From the main Posts screen in WordPress.org, find the post, hover your mouse over it, and click on **Quick Edit**. A quick editing area will appear where you can make tweaks to your post. Changes you can make include:

- Changing the title or slug.
- Amending the publication date.
- Assigning categories and tags (or removing them).
- Changing the status of the post to trash or draft, or making it private so only logged in authors, editors or admins can see it.

This feature is particularly handy if you've created a new category and want to assign it to some existing posts. Just go to the **Posts** screen and use quick edit on those posts to add the category.

In WordPress.com, you don't have access to the same quick editor, but you can access a few things from the main posts screen.

Click on **Blog Posts** in the admin menu and hover over the post. You'll be able to select from a few options, including:

- Editing (which opens the editing screen).
- Viewing the post in the live site.
- Viewing stats for that post.
- Viewing and managing the post's comments.
- Sharing the post.
- Copying it.
- Trashing it.

SHARING YOUR POSTS VIA SOCIAL MEDIA

Are you feeling like a bucket full of good ol' WordPress knowledge yet? We've covered a lot in this chapter, but that's for a good reason.

Posts are at the heart of WordPress. Understanding how to manage them will make your life easier and more efficient. So I hope you'll revisit this chapter in the future and use it for reference as you're creating your posts.

But before we go, I want to touch on sharing posts. If you're on WordPress.com or you're using the Jetpack plugin, you'll have your site hooked up to your social media accounts so that your posts will automatically be shared.

WordPress will automatically generate text for your social media posts. But I prefer to edit these, as the automatic text isn't always the most effective. In Twitter it'll just use the title of the post and in Facebook it'll use the opening lines from the post content. (I wish it would use the excerpt instead but it doesn't.)

To edit the text used in those social media posts while you're editing your post, click on the Jetpack icon above the **Publishing** tab on the right-hand side (it's a green circle with a lightning flash). Here you can turn off individual social media channels for your post if you want (handy if you want to manually tweet a link with hash-tags or mentions).

There's a field where you can customize your message. Type what you want to be shared to social media here and that's what will be broadcast instead of the default, along with a link to the post.

Alternatively, after you click the **Publish** button and before you click it again (when you're doing the pre-publish checks), there will be that same field for you to edit the text used when sharing the post.

But what if you want to bring your posts to life with some images and video? Read on, my friend. In the next chapter I'm going to take you on a guided tour of WordPress's media features.

23

IMAGES, VIDEO, DOWNLOADS AND MORE: ENHANCE YOUR SITE WITH MEDIA

WEBSITES AREN'T JUST about text!

Adding media to your website will make it more varied and engaging.

You can include images, video, downloads, slideshows, info-graphics—anything that will tell visitors about you and help you engage with readers.

WordPress gives you a Media section of the admin screens where you can upload and manage media, and you can also upload and embed media directly to your posts and pages.

Let's take a look at how it works.

EVERYTHING BUT THE KITCHEN SINK: MEDIA WORDPRESS WILL WORK WITH

WordPress gives you the ability to upload lots of different kinds of media, not just images (although if you're like me, it's images you'll be using the most).

These are the file types you can upload to WordPress:

- Images: jpg and png (jpg is good for photos, png for

graphics and anything with transparency such as an irregularly shaped logo).

- Files: Word documents, Excel spreadsheets (and the non-Microsoft equivalents), PDF files. If you want to upload a document or spreadsheet, I always recommend converting it to a PDF first. This way, it's harder for people to edit it. Even better is to include the content of your document in the body of a post. This is better for accessibility and for SEO.
- Video: just about any video file type is supported, although I'd recommend uploading your videos to a third-party service like YouTube and embedding them in your posts instead.
- Slideshows: PowerPoint, although you might want to upload slides to a service like Slideshare and embed them instead, as this can be more reliable.

UPLOAD YOUR MEDIA VIA THE MEDIA SCREENS

One way to upload media is via the Media section of the admin interface. You can also use this interface to work with images you've already uploaded, whether via these screens or directly into a post.

In both WordPress.com and WordPress.org, you have two Media screens: the Library and the screen for adding new media.

To upload media, just go to **Media > Add New** (or **Add** in WordPress.com) and upload your media file.

WordPress will ask you for metadata relating to your media; exactly what's needed will depend on the type of file. For images, it's important to add an ALT description as this is used by screen readers to describe the image to visitors with visual impairments. ALT descriptions are an important accessibility feature and may also enhance your SEO.

Once you've uploaded the media file, it's available in the media library so you can add it to a post or page, or you can use the link to its dedicated attachment page.

Once you've uploaded the media file, click the **Edit** link or button to edit it.

Image 23-1 The media editing screen

You can add a caption, which will appear below the image in posts, give it metadata such as the ALT text and a description for search engines, and see its attachment page link. WordPress automatically creates a dedicated attachment page for each media file, meaning you can view it on its own if you want. If you're reading the e-book version of this book and have clicked any of the links to images, then you'll have seen an attachment page in action.

UPLOAD MEDIA DIRECTLY TO A POST

99% of the time, I upload media directly to a post or page. This is for a very simple reason: that's where I want my image to show up!

To add a media item to a page or post, you create a media block. Image blocks let you add one image, while a gallery block lets you create a gallery of images.

You can then give the image(s) a caption, an ALT description and regular description (which is used by search engines), set what size you want to display it at and let it link to something if you want.

You can either link to the image file itself, to the attachment page, or to a custom link. This can be a page or post within your site, or elsewhere. So if you're including an image of your book, you might want to have it linking to somewhere people can buy it.

Image blocks give you lots of flexibility with the way you display images. You can set them to be centered or right- or left-aligned, meaning that the neighboring text will wrap around the image.

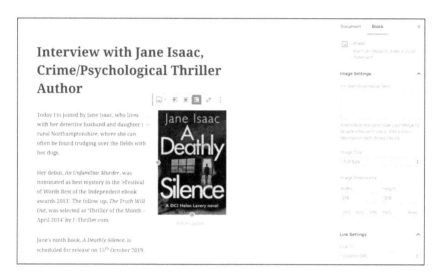

Image 23-2 A media block

You can also manually resize the image, so that it looks tidy when there's text wrapping around it. I like to check the value for the width in the **Block** pane on the right-hand side, and use a standard size for all my right- or left-aligned blocks. You don't have to do that, but I like to have a consistent layout across all my posts.

Once you've added an image block, you can edit it by clicking on the little pencil icon above it, switch it to align differently using the relevant icons next to that, or convert it to a different kind of media block such as a gallery block. You create a link for it in the **Blocks** pane on the right (*not* by clicking the pencil icon, which I have to admit took me a while to work out).

Links are useful when you're adding images of your books: you can link to the sales page.

USING FEATURED IMAGES

Featured images are a little bit different from standard images.

They're special images (the lucky things) that represent an individual post, and are displayed in the archive pages of your site (depending on your theme). They're also added to any Facebook posts or tweets you create to share the post.

To add a featured image to your post, go to the **Document** pane on the right of the post editing screen and click on **Set featured image**. You'll then be prompted to upload the image.

If you've got Jetpack installed and are sharing your posts to social media, WordPress will automatically attach the featured image to the tweet or Facebook update. Nice!

Image 23-3 A Facebook post displaying a featured image

Depending on your theme, the image will also be used in archive pages such as your main blog page and your category archives. The image shows up next to or below the post details (again depending on your theme) and acts as a link to the post.

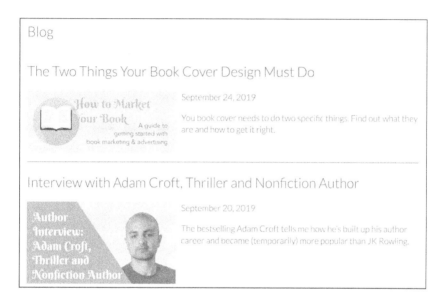

Image 23-4 An archive page with featured images

And that's not all! Your featured images like to keep themselves busy. If you're on WordPress.com (or you've got the Jetpack plugin), and you've enabled the Related Posts feature, you can opt to have featured images displayed there too. There's lots of evidence that people are much less likely to ignore a related post with an image, so it's something I recommend.

Image 23-5 Featured images for related posts

In summary, featured images are pretty cool. They liven up your website and encourage people to click through and read more content. I recommend adding them to all your posts.

ACTION! EMBEDDING VIDEO IN YOUR POSTS AND PAGES

So here's a conundrum. WordPress lets you upload all kinds of video files. But I've told you not to.

What should you do?

I think the answer is clear. Do as I say, of course!

OK, maybe I'm being unreasonable (and ever so slightly bossy). But there are legitimate reasons for embedding video instead of uploading it:

- Video files are big. If you upload a lot of them, you'll quickly fill up your allocation of server space and your hosting provider or the folks at WordPress.com will be getting in touch to politely suggest you give them more money for an upgrade.
- Video is notoriously unreliable when it comes to playback. Some devices (particularly iPhones and iPads) don't play all media types. You can't guarantee that the video file you've uploaded will be compatible with the device or computer your visitors are using.

- If you upload video to YouTube and stream it from there, you get extra Google juice. Google loooves video, mainly because it owns YouTube. If your videos are in YouTube as well as on your site, then you'll get twice the SEO benefits.

But I'm a busy writer, with beautiful words to squeeze out of my fevered brain. I don't have time to be faffing about with YouTube.

Yup, valid point. YouTube isn't something I devote a lot of time to, mainly because my target audience doesn't spend too much time on it.

But if you plan to add a significant amount of video to your website, it makes sense to upload it to YouTube first and then embed it into your post.

I'm not going to describe how to create a YouTube channel and upload videos to it here, as you'd be better off finding a ten-year-old and asking them. But if you don't have access to a ten-year-old, or your ten-year-old is one of those rare wonders who prefers to read than spend their time on YouTube, you can find instructions at wp4writers.com/youtube.

MASSIVE IMAGE FILES? HERE'S HOW TO FIX THAT

WordPress handles images in a way that's really clever: when you upload your file, it will create multiple versions of it: a thumbnail, a medium version and a large version, as well as your original. This means that when someone's viewing your image in a page or post, the appropriately-sized version of the image is loaded rather than your original, which may well be very big.

But sometimes your images are too big to be uploaded. Your hosting provider may have put a limit on upload file size, and your original image is too big.

If this happens, you'll get an error message. It'll probably say 'http error' or something like that.

If that happens, don't panic.

Start by making the image smaller. Use your image software to reduce the size to 2400 pixels by 2400 pixels or similar (if your image isn't square, these won't be the correct dimensions, but 2400 pixels maximum along the longest side allows for displaying the image on high resolution screens and isn't as big as your original might be).

Then try uploading it again.

If it still doesn't work, you may have used up your server space. It happens, especially when a site has been running for a little while. Raise a support ticket with your hosting provider if you've got a self-hosted site, or upgrade to a higher plan if you're on WordPress.com.

You can also edit your image files right within the WordPress admin screens, after uploading them.

Find the image in your post or via the media library, and click on **Edit image** to see its editing screen. Here you have the option to delete it, add a caption and other metadata, and to crop or resize it.

To crop the image, just drag your mouse around the portion of the image you want to keep and click the crop button to the top left of the image. Then click the **Save** button.

You can also edit the size and aspect ratio using the controls on the right-hand side of the screen.

Another nifty feature that is quite recent is to be able to resize your image as it appears on the screen, by resizing it within its block.

To do this, you need to be in the editing screen for the post or page where the image is displayed. Go to the image block and select it. Blue dots will appear on the edges of the image. Drag these in and out to resize the image. WordPress will not only change the image that appears on the page, but it will also generate a version of the file that's the right size when it's viewed in a browser, which speeds things up for your site visitors. Clever, huh?

GIVE YOUR MEDIA EXTRA ATTENTION WITH METADATA

I've already mentioned metadata, but it's something that's easy to overlook.

Metadata is data about data; in this case, it's data about your image.

WordPress gives you the option to amend the following meta-data about your images:

- A caption: this will appear on the page beneath the image and tells readers more about it.
- Alternative text (also known as ALT text): used by screen readers to tell visitors with visual impairments what's in the photo. If you want your site to be accessible, you should add ALT text to every image.
- Description: this will be displayed by search engines if your image comes up in a search. It can be useful for SEO.

Adding metadata to your images has accessibility, SEO and usability benefits. It takes a few extra seconds but if it helps get your website (and your books) out to a wider audience, it's worth doing.

So you have some wonderful posts. They're entertaining, and informative, and they're going to make it irresistible for anyone who reads them to become your biggest fan.

Not if you don't tell anyone, they won't. Which why in the next chapter, we're looking at ways to share your content.

DON'T KEEP IT TO YOURSELF:
SHARING CONTENT

You've written the world's best blog post.

It's a literary marvel, full of wise and witty insights. You're exceptionally proud of it, and think it will convince people that you're a literary genius and they simply have to buy your book.

So you publish it to your website, and then…

Then what?

If you just leave it sitting there, how many people do you think will find it? Not very many. Which is why you need to share your content.

WHY SHARE CONTENT?

I'm going to start with something really fundamental here.

If you're an author and you want to reach an audience, you need to use social media.

I'm not saying you have to spend your every waking moment on Facebook, or tweet a hundred times a day, or upload every photo you ever take to Instagram.

Far from it. In fact, if you do those things, you'll waste a lot of time.

For tips on how to use social media as an author, including being strategic and making sure you aren't wasting your time, go to wp4writers.com/socialmedia.

If you do decide to use social media (and I'd recommend it), there are two ways in which your social media accounts will interact with your website:

- You'll share your website content via your social media accounts.
- You'll encourage people visit your site to share your content via their own social media accounts.

The first of these will help expand the reach of your blog posts in particular. People will be able to follow you on Twitter or like your Facebook page, and when you post something new, they'll get a notification.

My blog gets a spike in traffic every time I publish a new post. And at least half of that traffic comes directly from Facebook or Twitter. That's because I share my posts, and I do it without lifting a finger (yay!).

The second acts as a form of social proof. Content that is shared on someone else's social media account and not just your own carries the weight of their recommendation. It's a powerful way of getting noticed.

Social Proof for Authors

You may have heard the term 'social proof' being bandied about a lot in author circles, and it might be one of those phrases that makes you shudder. After all, it's got a nasty, marketing-speak, even spammy, ring to it.

But social proof is really important to authors. Social proof happens every time someone else spreads the word about your books. It isn't confined to social media: the good old word-of-mouth book recommendation is a form of social proof, and we've been doing that since the invention of the printing press.

Other examples of social proof for your work include book reviews and recommendations, comments on the adverts for your books, people passing a copy of your book to their friends, and every time someone mentions you or your books online or in person. Without social proof, most authors wouldn't have a career.

These two forms of sharing content from your website will help you get more visitors and hopefully more signups to your mailing list. But you don't want to spend all your time logging in and out of social media accounts and manually linking to your content. Nor do you want to ask people to share your content for fear of coming across as pushy.

The good news is that WordPress automates both of these processes for you.

Let's take a look at how you set it up, starting with sharing to your own social media accounts.

WHERE TO SHARE CONTENT

Everywhere! I hear you cry.

Well, no.

Sharing too widely will make you come across as spammy.

You should share your content via your own social media accounts, and via other groups, pages or message boards *that allow self-promotion.*

That last line is crucial. Don't ever share content to a Facebook group, or a LinkedIn page, or anywhere else, that doesn't allow self-promotion. I'm a member of multiple Facebook groups for authors and most of them don't allow self-promo. On some of them, if you promote yourself you will be banned instantly. No appeal. You're simply out on your ear.

So if a group doesn't explicitly say that it allows promotion, assume it doesn't. Check with the administrator before posting anything promotional, and engage with the group first anyway.

If in doubt, don't share your content on someone else's space. Become active instead; build up a reputation as someone who wants to engage and help people. That way, you won't annoy people if and when you do eventually promote yourself.

Phew! Rant over. Got the message?

Good. So let's get on to where you can (and should) be sharing your posts: your own Twitter and Facebook accounts.

SHARE YOUR POSTS TO FACEBOOK AND TWITTER WITHOUT LIFTING A FINGER

Sharing content should be part of a wider social media strategy that is aimed at engaging with readers, building a following, and not being spammy.

I'm not going to get into that here (I may write a whole other book on the subject as it's a big one), but what I will say is that posting links to your own content is a fine and valid way of raising the profile of your author website. It's even more effective if that's not the only thing you share; but even if you don't spend any time on Twitter or Facebook at all, I recommend sharing your posts.

And the great news is that you can get WordPress to do it for you every time you publish a new post, without lifting a finger.

If you're on WordPress.com, this is already part of your package, even if you have a free account (yay!). If you've got a self-hosted WordPress site, you'll need to download and install the Jetpack plugin, which gives you all the features of WordPress.com on your self-hosted site.

So, you got the plugin? Activated it and ready to go? Excellent (I felt a shiver run down my spine then as I imagined *The Simpsons'* Montgomery Burns breathing down my neck). Let's get started.

SHARING POSTS ON WORDPRESS.COM

WordPress.com has a feature called Publicize that lets you automatically share all of your new posts to your social media accounts.

All you need to do is link your website to your social media and then leave it to do its magic.

To set it up, go to **Configure > Sharing**. The **Connections** tab will open, giving you a choice of social media platforms.

Next to each one you want to share your posts to (i.e. each one you have an account with), click the **Connect** button.

WordPress will then walk you through the process of connecting to your social media account and authorizing the connection.

Work through this process for each of the social media accounts you want to connect.

Once you've done that, you'll find that you can control the sharing of each blog post when you're creating or editing it. Open up one of your existing blog posts (or create a new one) and click on the Jetpack icon on the top right, above the settings (it's a little green circle with a lightning flash in it).

You'll see a **Share this post** section, with a list of the social media accounts that you've connected. You can toggle any of these on or off, and you can also edit the text which will be posted to your social media accounts with the link.

If you don't edit this text and keep all of your accounts toggled to on, WordPress will just automatically use your post title (on Twitter) or the opening sentences of your post (on Facebook) and share that with a link. So you don't have to do anything. Just sit on your chaise longue and eat chocolates. Nice.

SHARING POSTS ON WORDPRESS.ORG

The process for WordPress.org is similar, as you're using the WordPress.com Publicize feature via the Jetpack plugin.

In the admin screens, click on **Jetpack > Settings**. Click the **Sharing** tab.

Toggle the **Automatically share your posts to social**

media accounts button to on and click on the **Connect your social media accounts** link.

Connect with your social media accounts in the same way described above for WordPress.com.

Every time you publish a post, WordPress will run you through a pre-publication check. An element of this is focused on sharing your posts. You can toggle individual social media accounts on and off and you can also edit the text that's displayed in your social share along with the link. If you don't edit this, Twitter will display the post title plus a link and Facebook will display the opening lines of the post plus a link. Neither of these is ideal (one's too short, the other is too long and random), so I recommend typing in custom text which will be shared on social media.

SHARE POSTS WITH THE WORDPRESS.COM COMMUNITY

On WordPress.com (and with Jetpack enabled in WordPress.org), you also have access to the WordPress.com community. This means other users with a WordPress.com account can follow your blog and comment on your posts.

You can make this easier by adding a Subscribe widget to your sidebar.

In WordPress.com, click on **Customize** and then **Widgets**. Select the sidebar widget area and add the **Follow Blog** widget.

In a self-hosted site, you can access widgets via the Customizer or by clicking on **Appearance > Widgets**. Select the **Blog Subscriptions (Jetpack)** widget and add that to your sidebar.

Once people subscribe to your site, they'll get an email every time you publish a new post, so they won't miss a thing.

SOCIAL PROOF: LET READERS SHARE YOUR POSTS WITH SHARING BUTTONS

I've already said that having other people share your content is much more powerful than sharing your own. It's a form of social proof.

Imagine you're at a party. You've taken a copy of your book along in the hope it'll come up in conversation and you'll be able to show it to people; you might even be able to sell it. But now imagine someone else walks into the room carrying a copy of your book. They start telling people how much they enjoyed it.

How would that make you feel?

If you're anything like me, someone would be peeling you off the floor. And you'd have an ear-to-ear grin.

Well, social sharing is a bit like that. Instead of (or more accurately, as well as) you sharing your own content, other people share it with their networks.

You want people to do that? Of course you do. And you can make it easier for them by adding social sharing buttons to your posts.

ADDING SOCIAL SHARING ON WORDPRESS.COM

WordPress lets you add social sharing buttons to every post in your site. These are buttons that let people share the post they're reading to their own social media account.

To set it up, go to **Configure > Sharing > Sharing Buttons**. Scroll down to the **Options** section to specify which post types you want to add sharing buttons to. WordPress will add them to posts and pages by default, but I prefer to turn them off for pages.

Scroll back up to configure how the buttons will look and which social media sites they'll include. Click on **Edit sharing buttons** to change the buttons and reorder them. Just click on the buttons you want, to toggle them on or off. To change the order, click the **Reorder** button and drag them around until you're happy.

You can also change the appearance of the buttons, to include just an icon, icons and text, text only, or the official buttons for each social media platform.

As well as buttons for the social media platforms, there are two options which are specific to WordPress.com: the **Reblog** button and the **Like** button.

The **Reblog** button gives people the option to share your content to their own blog. It's attributed to you and includes a link back to your original blog post. This can be a great way to grow your reach, although be wary of it if you're concerned about copyright and/or plagiarism (although to be honest, worrying about those when it comes to your blog is about worrying that the tide might come in and soak your shoes if you stand too close to the sea).

The **Like** button gives other WordPress users the opportunity to like your content, and will help with social proof inside the WordPress ecosystem. With millions of blogs on WordPress.com and hundreds of thousands of users, it can't do any harm to have that as an option.

Once you're happy with your settings, click the **Save Changes** button and you're good to go. Social sharing buttons will now appear on all of your posts.

Image 24-1 Social sharing buttons on a blog post

ADDING SOCIAL SHARING ON WORDPRESS.ORG

This is another time you're going to need the Jetpack plugin (my favorite plugin, remember?).

To set this up on a self-hosted WordPress site, go to **Jetpack > Settings**. Select the **Sharing** tab.

You'll see a section for sharing buttons. Toggle it on and click the **Configure your sharing buttons** link. Now follow the instructions above as for WordPress.com.

Once you've got those two features set up, you can forget about them. Focus on creating your content and making it as good as possible. WordPress will automatically share your posts to your social media accounts and give visitors the option to share it to theirs. Sweet!

But there is another way to attract more visitors to your site, and that's by making sure people can find you via search engines. You work on this by installing and configuring an SEO plugin, which is covered in the next chapter.

SEARCH ENGINE OPTIMIZATION

YOU WANT people to find your website. Otherwise you wouldn't go to the trouble of setting one up.

I've already talked about some of the ways you can help people to find your site, including via social media shares. In the next part of this book, I'll show you how to help people who've read your books to find your site.

But here we're focusing on grabbing potential readers who are already on the internet. And the technique we're going to be using is search engine optimization, or SEO.

BENEFITS OF SEO

To some people, SEO is a dirty word.

It makes you think of dodgy websites crammed full of keywords. Of less than reputable internet marketing companies telling you they can get you to the top of the search engine rankings if you pay them three hundred and seventy-two dollars a week.

But the good news is that good SEO isn't like this. The search engines, and Google in particular, have developed to the point where the people who benefit the most from the way the algorithms work is folks like you and me: writers.

Whoa, hold on there, just what is an algorithm?

Good question. An algorithm is code that helps a search engine to work out what someone searching for a given term would like to be shown in the search results.

So if you search for 'kayaking in Outer Mongolia', Google wants to give you the highest quality results for that search.

And quality isn't just about keywords. I could write a post entitled 'Kayaking in Outer Mongolia' and I could just repeat the words 'kayaking in Outer Mongolia' again and again in the body of the post. You'd soon get bored (I am already). And you wouldn't come back to my website in a hurry.

Google wants to give you results that are high quality; that you will find useful. And its algorithms are what enable it to do that. They look not just at the words in your search, but at other related words, at the length of the post, the number of times it's been linked to or visited, and lots of other factors which are kept very secret. It's the algorithm that has made Google the behemoth it is today.

If you optimize your website for SEO, you will get higher ranking in search results for terms that are relevant to your website and your writing.

So let's say someone's looking for tips on basket weaving. You just happen to have written a book on the subject, and you've been blogging about it.

When someone types *basket weaving* into Google, there's a good chance your blog will come up in the search results. They'll then click on the link to your post, read it, decide they simply have to read more, and buy your book.

For nonfiction authors, this is particularly powerful, as people are much more likely to search for advice or information via Google than they are for stories. But spending a bit of time optimizing your site if you're a fiction author is worth it—just don't spend too much time on it.

Let's take a look at a couple of examples from my own experience. I write psychological thrillers and books on self-publishing. Using the Google keyword planner (wp4writers.com/googleads), I've been able to find that 100 to 1,000 searches a month are made for *psychological thriller books*, while 1,000 to 10,000 searches a month are made for *self-publishing*. That's ten times as many.

Should I research keywords?

I can recommend using the Google keyword planner to identify words people might search for that are relevant to your books. But keywords aren't everything, and please, *please* don't stuff your content full of them.

So, if your site is optimized for the search terms people are likely to use when looking for the topic you write about, then it will help you be found.

But this isn't about filling your posts with keywords: quite the opposite. Read on for more SEO tips.

CONTENT AND SEO

The Google algorithm is designed to find good stuff; high quality content that people will find engaging.

And quality content has two main attributes:

- It's authoritative (or entertaining if that's its function).
- It's well-written.

Authoritative or entertaining content is written by people who know their topic or who know how to entertain. And well-written content is written by… writers.

So you're at an automatic advantage.

Google crawls millions, if not billions, of web pages every day. And it learns from doing that.

One of the things it learns is the vocabulary surrounding a given topic. Google knows that an authoritative post on a subject, written by someone who knows their onions, will contain not just the search term you might be optimizing for, but other related words too. So if you *are* writing about growing onions, then your posts will probably contain other words like soil, dig, allium, harvest, and other words I don't know because I don't grow onions.

So don't worry about putting one keyword or phrase into your posts again and again. Instead, relax. Trust your knowledge of what you're writing about, and focus on writing quality content. That will be just as valuable as stuffing the word 'onions' into your post twenty times. In fact, if you do use one phrase too often, it will actually have a negative impact on your search ranking, as Google will think you're trying to game the system.

So write quality, engaging, entertaining and informative content. It will not only help your search engine rankings, but it will also encourage people to browse your site and buy your books.

WORDPRESS AND SEO

WordPress is already pretty good for SEO out of the box. Search engines like sites that are well coded and efficient. WordPress has fairly clean code, its code is structured in a way that the search engines can understand, and if you have WordPress.com or a self-hosted site with a quality hosting provider, it will be fast.

These give you an automatic boost before you even think about SEO.

But what else can you do to enhance your search rankings?

INSTALLING AND CONFIGURING AN SEO PLUGIN

If you're running a self-hosted site, you can install a free SEO plugin to give you more SEO options and help you rank more highly.

If you're using WordPress.com, you'll have to upgrade to a premium plan to benefit from SEO options. To be honest, I think you'd be better off paying for hosting instead and getting yourself a self-hosted site (you can find out how to make the switch in Chapter 19).

So here, I'm just going to show you how to install and configure a SEO plugin for a self-hosted site. If you do want to stick with WordPress.com, and are happy paying the extra money for a premium account, you can find out about SEO for WordPress.com at wp4writers.com/wpseo.

CHOOSING A SEO PLUGIN

There are a number of great free SEO plugins available for Word-Press. The one I recommend is called All in One SEO Pack. It was one of the first powerful SEO plugins, it has a ton of useful features, is easy to set up, and has everything you'll need for an author website without upgrading to the premium version.

Someone told me that SEO by Yoast is the most popular SEO plugin. Why aren't you recommending that?

It's true that WordPress SEO by Yoast is the most popular SEO plugin. I've used it on a number of sites, and in all cases, I've eventually migrated to using another SEO plugin instead. I think its faults outweigh its undeniable power as a plugin.

Firstly, it can be buggy. Upgrading the plugin has caused my clients' websites to crash on multiple occasions; not something I was happy about, as I'm sure you can imagine. It's one of those plugins I would never upgrade immediately, as it takes time for the developers to fix bugs. I don't think that's good enough.

Secondly, I hate the interface. It throws popups at you non-stop, trying to tell you what to do and encourage you to upgrade to the premium version. If you don't know about SEO, these popups will just be confusing and irritating, and will distract you from working through the plugin settings at your own pace.

So if you do decide to install WordPress SEO by Yoast, go ahead, but don't say I didn't warn you.

The All In One SEO Pack (my, that's a mouthful) plugin is free and you install it in just the same way as you would any other plugin.

Once you've done that, activate it and you'll be taken to the settings screens. If you aren't taken to the settings screens, you'll see a new link in your admin menu on the left called **All in One SEO**. Click on that.

SEO CONFIGURATION

Let's start by configuring the All In One SEO Pack plugin.

Go to the Plugins screen and find the All In One SEO Pack plugin. Click **Activate**.

You'll be taken to a setup screen with some information on the plugin. At the bottom of this screen is a link to continue with setup. Click on it.

You'll now be presented with the settings screen for the plugin. The exact configuration is up to you, but here's what I recommend:

- **General Settings**: Leave all of these as they are.
- **Home Page Settings—Home Page Title**: This is the title for your home page in search results. Type in the name and tagline of your site here.
- **Home Page Settings—Home Page Description**:

Type in the description you want for your home page. This is what will be seen on a search page after someone has searched for your site. So it needs to encourage people to click through to the site. Make it short, snappy and engaging.

- **Use Static Front Page instead**: Ignore this, as you've already configured it in site settings.
- **Title Settings**: Leave all these as they are.
- **Content Type Settings**: Leave this with just **Posts** and **Pages** checked. You don't want search engines crawling anything else.
- **Display Settings**: Again, leave this with just **Posts** and **Pages** checked.
- **Webmaster Verification**: Ignore this section, it's no longer necessary to verify your site with search engines as they will crawl it automatically.
- **Google Settings**: If this section is still there when you read this, ignore it! It relates to Google+, which is becoming defunct as I write.
- **Noindex Settings**: This tells search engines which pages in your site to crawl so they can show up in search results. Check the following for both **Default to NOINDEX** and **Default to NOFOLLOW**: **Media, User Requests, oEmbed Responses, Blocks** (don't worry if any of these aren't present for your site). This means that the only content type which *aren't* checked are **Posts** and **Pages**.
- **Noindex Settings**, individual settings: There will be a series of checkboxes allowing you to set Noindex for different content types. Check them all. (Noindex means the search engines don't index these pages: there are some content types you don't want the search engines to focus on.)
- **Advanced Settings**: Ignore this section. For more advanced SEO, you might want to come back later and specify individual posts or pages that you don't want

search engines to index in the **Exclude Pages** field, but you can also do this when editing the individual post or page.

- **Keyword Settings**: Leave **Disabled** selected. Adding keywords to pages are no longer useful for SEO and you don't need to waste time with them.

Once you've done all that, click the **Update Options** button.

You still have a couple of things to do. In the admin menu, click **All in One SEO > Feature Manager**.

You'll see a list of extra features you can add to the plugin. Some of these are included in the free version, others are premium.

Activate the following:

- XML Sitemaps.
- Social Meta.
- Robots.txt.
- Performance.

Note: The Performance feature can help boost performance in a way that helps your SEO. If you want to improve your site's performance even more, install a performance plugin. There's more about those in Chapter 38.

You don't need to do anything to configure these features: they'll be set up for you.

These will all provide search engines with more information about your site that will help them index it, identify what's there, and find it when people do a search.

Well done! You've configured your SEO plugin.

OPTIMIZING CONTENT FOR SEO

So, you've got your SEO plugin configured and you're ready for hordes of visitors to start finding you via Google.

Errr, it's not as easy as that. Sorry!

The SEO plugin is a tool that can help you to optimize your content for SEO, but you still have to spend some time doing it.

There are two aspects to this: the content itself, and the metadata such as post descriptions and image descriptions. We've already looked at how writing great, relevant content will boost your SEO above. Now let's take a look at the nuts and bolts of how you can use metadata to boost your SEO.

OPTIMIZING POSTS

First up, posts. If you're running a blog, this will be the primary way that people find you. You'll write a blog post that answers a burning question, someone will google that question, and lo and behold, your post will appear in their search results.

If you write nonfiction, this is especially powerful, but don't dismiss it for fiction.

You can do this in the editing screen for each individual post and page.

Once you've written your post or page, scroll down to the bottom of the screen.

You'll see the following SEO options:

- A preview of what your post will look like in search results.
- A **Title** field, which defaults to your post title.
- A **Description** field, which will be displayed below the title in search results.
- Options for Noindexing, Nofollowing and disabling this post. Unless you don't want Google finding this post, ignore these.

I recommend editing the title and adding a better description. But what do you type? How do you maximize that Google juice and get those flocks of visitors to your site? Here are my tips:

- The SEO Title should be no more than 60 characters long, preferably less. Keep it short and snappy. Try to use words that someone might plug into a search. So for a hypothetical post on setting up a mailing list in MailChimp, I might use 'Create a MailChimp mailing list for your newsletter'. Note that that has the terms *MailChimp*, *mailing list* and *newsletter*, all of which are likely to be searched on.
- The SEO Description can be up to 160 characters long. It's more descriptive and designed to encourage people to click through to the post. So I might use 'Learn how to create a mailing list and reach potential readers using MailChimp, for authors and writers'. This includes the terms *readers*, *authors* and *writers*, as that's my target market.

Once you've typed in a title or description, publish your post. You've increased its chances of ranking higher in search results.

If you've already published some posts and not optimized them for SEO, take the time to go back over them and add a description and title for SEO. Without this, there is no benefit to having a SEO plugin installed: the whole point is that it gives you these fields.

OPTIMIZING MEDIA

Now let's take a look at how you optimize media. This is a little easier as it comes baked into WordPress itself. And you can do it in both WordPress.org and WordPress.com (hurray!).

To add metadata to an image, you need to open the editing screen for that image:

- In WordPress.org, go to **Media > Library**. If you see a

list of images with text, find the image you want and next to it, click the **Edit** link. If instead you're looking at a grid of images, click the image to see the Attachment Details screen, then click the **Edit more details** link towards the bottom right. Or you can toggle between list view and grid view in the media library by clicking the icons above the images.

- In WordPress.com, click the **Media** link in the admin menu. Select the image you want to edit, then click the **Edit** button above the images.

You'll now be presented with the media editing screen. You've got four items of metadata you can edit:

- **Title**: defaults to the filename. If this is gobbledygook, change it to something that makes sense. So my snapshot of a cute cat, originally called *DESC89979*, can become *cute-cat*. I normally change the name of the file before uploading it so it's optimized.
- **Caption**: This is text that appears on the post or page along with the image. Leave it blank if you don't want any text appearing with the image.
- **Alt text**: This will enhance accessibility as it's read out by screen readers used by people with visual impairments who can't see your images. Here you should describe your image. So I might use *a small ginger cat yawning and stretching her legs while looking into the camera, lying on a purple cushion*. Sounds like this cat is having a great day!
- **Description**: Google will use this for searching images. So instead of being descriptive, use words that someone might search for.

Once you've done this, click **Update** to save changes if you're in WordPress.org. If you're using WordPress.com, click **Done**.

When searching for images, Google will use the image description as well as the text on the page that it's embedded in. So don't try gaming the search results by sticking cat images in your posts about nuclear physics, in the hope that you'll attract nuclear physicists who also like cats. Unless that is your very specific niche. I wish you luck with that.

But there's more to writing content than just targeting the search engines. Good content will not only attract new visitors to your site, it will also encourage them to keep reading, to sign up to your newsletter, and to buy your books.

Read on to find out about how you can develop a content strategy (sounds highfalutin', I know, but bear with me) can help you do that.

CONTENT STRATEGY

OK, so that's the nuts and bolts of SEO over with. I hope you're now planning to go out and set up your own sleazy SEO outfit so you can con millions of unwitting authors into parting with their cash. Or not, as the case may be.

Now for something a little more fun (well, I think it's fun, but I may be a bit sad): content strategy.

Content strategy is an important part of your SEO efforts. It also links to your goal of reaching more readers and engaging with them. It will help you build an army of superfans and sign more people up to your mailing list.

Bold claims, I know. Let me enlighten you as to how it works, and you can decide for yourself.

IDENTIFYING YOUR CONTENT GOALS

Your website should link to your goals as an author. Some people have very well-defined author goals. They want to sell a certain number of books, reach number 1 on the NYT charts, or get a publishing deal with Penguin Random House. Others just want to write.

Which is admirable, and what it really comes down to for all of us. My goal is to earn a living from my writing. This links to the 'just want to write' goal, as if I can make a living writing, I don't have to spend time doing other things that aren't as much fun but are a necessary money-making evil. We all have bills to pay, after all.

But for me to make a success of my author career, I need more specific goals. And so do you.

So before you start writing lots of content, think about these questions:

- What kind of thing do you write? What's the tone? This should carry across to your blog.
- Who is your ideal reader? Please don't say everyone. If you aim for everyone, you'll appeal to no one. Identify a few things your ideal reader will enjoy apart from your writing.
- What do you enjoy writing about?
- What topics will your ideal reader enjoy reading about or find useful? This might be hints and tips related to the topic of your nonfiction, or facts and anecdotes that are relevant to your fiction (if you write spy novels, find out interesting facts about real life espionage; if you write historical romance, share stories of real-life historical romances, or examples of the restrictions lovers might have faced in years gone by).
- What can you write about that will entice readers and encourage them to read your books? Character bios, excerpts, related short stories?

Think as well about how much you can realistically write. Posting once a week works well for many authors, but if that's too much for you, post once a fortnight instead. A regular stream of posts will keep the search engines happy (Google likes fresh content), give you things to share on social media, and help your readers know when to expect something new from you.

IDENTIFYING WHAT CONTENT APPEALS TO YOUR READERS

The first thing is to consider what content your readers will enjoy. There are two ways to do this: by looking at data, and by asking them.

As you create more content for your site, you'll be able to look at your site stats (which you can access directly in WordPress.com or by adding the Jetpack plugin to Wordpress.org) and use that to identify which kinds of post are getting the most views and comments.

You might also want to do some keyword research, and identify which search terms people are looking for that are relevant to your blog. This will apply most to nonfiction authors. Check out Chapter 25 on SEO for more.

But this isn't limited to your blog posts. Look at your newsletters and your social media posts. What are people most likely to respond to? What fuels debate? Chances are if you write more of this kind of content, you'll get more engagement from readers. And more engagement means more newsletter signups, more fans, and ultimately more book sales.

AVOIDING BLOGGER'S BLOCK

The biggest stumbling block for many blogs is running out of steam. When you start your blog you're all fired up, full of energy and content ideas. But over time, other things will get in the way and you'll find yourself struggling to think of things to write about.

If this happens, don't despair. No one will hate you if you miss the occasional blog post. But you can take steps to avoid this. One is to resist the temptation to publish new content as frequently as you'd like when you first start your blog. Instead, write some of those posts and schedule them for the future. That way, when you run out of ideas or time, you have something you can publish all ready for you. Identify a realistic publishing schedule and stick to that right from the start. So if you think you can publish once a week in the long term but have enough ideas for two posts a week at the beginning, go ahead and write them, but schedule them for a few months ahead. That way, you'll never have a week with nothing to publish.

You can also cheat. Yes, I said you can cheat.

There is a way to produce content that involves you doing very little work, and in my experience, it produces some of the most popular content. That method is interviews.

I publish an interview with a fellow author every week on my site rachelmcwrites.com. I don't sit down and talk with those authors, because they're busy people. Instead, I send them a Word document with the questions, normally about a month in advance, and they fill it out in their own time. Once I receive the answers back, I copy them to a new post in my site, add some photos and links and schedule it for the next available slot.

Authors love the opportunity to be interviewed. It expands their platform and raises their profile with my website visitors, and increases my audience because they often send their followers to the interview. It also provides regular varied content looking at writing and publishing from a range of perspectives. And compared to a full-length blog post, it takes me very little time to do.

Now, I know some of those authors are reading this book, and I'd like to take the opportunity here to thank them for their contribution. This is not *just* a cheat's way of adding more content to my blog: it's turning into a really valuable resource for my readers, sand something I couldn't do without them. (Thanks, authors!)

But you could do something similar. If you write fiction, you could interview experts in fields related to your stories. If you write nonfiction, you could interview other experts in your field or related fields. It won't diminish your authority; it'll enhance it. And it'll increase your audience significantly.

An alternative to interviews is guest posts. I write guest posts for a range of blogs (some of which I'm paid for, some not), and accept guest posts for my own blog. It's another way of getting a greater variety of content on your blog, and won't take you a lot of time.

CREATING A CONTENT PLAN

It's also sensible to create a content plan. This will be a list of the topics you plan to write about over the next few weeks. It helps you plan your workload and identify any posts for which you'll have to do research in advance, or gather assets.

If you want to be really organized, you can use a task management tool like Trello to manage your publishing workflow (it can be useful for books too), but if you're like me, you'll want to keep things simpler. A notebook will suffice, with a list of topics and dates.

Don't worry if your plan goes awry occasionally. Sometimes you'll add an unscheduled post because something comes up that you just have to write about right now, or you'll drop a topic because you don't have enough material.

It's fine. It's just a blog. If you have to tweak things in order to stay sane and keep aside time for writing, so be it. But a schedule will help you pick up again when things get back to normal, and avoid the all-too-common scenario of one missed blog post leading to another, then another, until you decide there's not much point writing any more.

BATCHING AND SCHEDULING

You can use the scheduling feature in WordPress to write a post and schedule it for a later date. It'll be published on that date without you having to lift a finger (see Chapter 22 for guidance on how to do it).

Scheduling is one of my favorite WordPress features. It means I can set aside a day to write a bunch of posts and then schedule them for the next few weeks. Then I can get back to writing the next book.

If you decide you want to publish something else on a date you already had something scheduled for, it's easy to change the scheduled date and push it back. As long as the post hasn't been published yet, the choice is yours.

MONITORING AUDIENCE ENGAGEMENT

Your blog is designed to engage with your audience. Its job is to attract people to your site, to keep them there, and then to funnel them into signing up for your newsletter.

But how do you know if it's doing that?

By monitoring your site stats.

In WordPress.com, or in WordPress.org with the Jetpack plugin, you have access to information about how many visitors your site got on a given day, week or month, and how many times each post and page has been viewed.

It's worth taking the time to interrogate this information every few weeks or months, depending on how often you blog and how much time you have available (I know you're busy producing your magnum opus, after all).

Look at the data and ask yourself:

- On what days of the week does my site get the most traffic? Is it when I add new content, or not?
- Where is my traffic coming from? Social media, search, or direct? If it's search, what are the search terms?
- What are the most popular posts? What do they have in common?
- What are the least popular posts? What do they have in common?

What your posts have in common might not just be the content. It might be the length of the post, the inclusion of images and other media, the time of day when you published it, or anything else. Try to identify what makes a popular post in your blog, and produce more posts like that. For those posts that are unpopular, identifying what makes them so will help you avoid wasting time writing more content like that.

Of course there will be some content you write for your own enjoyment and edification. Nothing wrong with that. But if your blog's purpose is to engage with an audience, then you need to know what that audience wants.

So that's content covered! I hope you're now armed with a gazillion ideas for blog posts, and raring to start writing.

But hold on. All that lovely content needs to serve a purpose. And in my opinion, one of the main purposes of your website should be to encourage people to sign up for your mailing list.

In the next section of the book, we'll look at how you can integrate your mailing list with your website, whether you're on Word-Press.com or WordPress.org, and let it work for you while you're busy elsewhere.

VI

ADDING NEWSLETTER SIGNUPS TO YOUR SITE

THE IMPORTANCE OF NEWSLETTER SIGNUPS

YOU NOW HAVE A WORKING WEBSITE. You've signed up for Word-Press.com or WordPress.org, you've installed a theme, set things up and started adding some content.

Now for the important stuff. The most useful thing your website can do is hoover up newsletter subscribers, so you can keep in touch with readers and sell them books (amongst other things).

In the next few chapters of this book, you'll learn how to do it.

ARE YOU STILL HERE?

You're still reading? You're not rubbing your hands in glee at the thought of all those lovely people buying your books?

So you need a bit more persuading. Maybe you already have a website and are happy using it to provide information about your books. Maybe you're a bit scared of the work that maintaining a newsletter will involve.

I hear you. Read on and I'll try to convince you.

THE POWER OF A NEWSLETTER

In this book, I've already talked about how a self-hosted WordPress site has many benefits over WordPress.com, and that one of them is the fact that the website is yours. It's your code, your content, your server space (well, the server space you rent, but your hosting provider has no claim over your actual site). Not to mention your domain name.

A newsletter is similar.

Put your hand up if you've been using a Facebook page to communicate with your readers (I see you at the back).

That's good. Facebook is a great place to engage with readers. But have you noticed that in the last couple of years, it's become harder to get your updates seen by your fans? You put all that effort into winning page likes, and then those people who liked your page because they want to hear from you... well, they aren't even seeing your updates in their news feed.

That's because Facebook wants you to pay to boost posts. So instead of delivering your posts to your fans, it suggests you might want to hand over some of your hard-earned cash to ensure they see them.

Sounds like a con, huh?

It isn't. Facebook owns the platform. They own the data. They have control. They can do what the hell they like with your posts. If they choose to show them to no one at all (and it happens), that's up to them.

It sucks.

You may have experienced something similar with Amazon. You put all that effort into adding metadata to your books in the KDP dashboard (or your publisher did). You ran adverts targeting books you wanted in your also-boughts list (if you don't know what also-bought are, check out wp4writers.com/also-boughts). You even ran newsletter swaps. But now, Amazon doesn't even show people those also-boughts (at least not in the USA). All that effort, wasted! (Not quite wasted, Amazon will still use that data to recommend your books, but still.)

Amazon can do this, because it's their platform. They want to encourage you (or your publisher) to advertise in order to increase your books' visibility. You may have heard the term 'pay-to-play' being used a lot recently, and this is what it means.

So you need a way of reaching your readers over which you have control. A means of going directly to them, using a set of data you own.

Your newsletter is just that. Although you use a mailing list provider to make it work, the data is yours. You can download a list of your subscribers at any time (I recommend doing it regularly), and it gives you direct access to their inbox. If you make sure they add you to their contacts list, you can be sure it'll get through.

Many authors swear by their mailing list. For some, it's made their career. Personally I have separate mailing lists for my fiction and nonfiction readers (you can sign up to my nonfiction list and get my free book *Author Website Blueprint* at rachelmcwrites.com/ blueprint). I mail each of them every week, which is the frequency that gets the most response. You don't have to do that. You could just email them when you have a book out. Or something in between.

It's up to you. But a mailing list will give you direct access to your readers in a way no other platform will. And with some providers, until you have a threshold of people on your list, it's free.

Have I convinced you? Then read on.

NEWSLETTER OPTIONS

So you've decided to get yourself an author newsletter. Wise choice.

But where to start?

The first thing is to decide which provider to use. There are a few of them, which I'll provide details of in this chapter.

But before you read that, there's one important thing to consider, which is this:

If you're on WordPress.com, the only mailing list provider you can link to easily and for free is MailChimp.

That may help you decide on MailChimp. Or it may put you off WordPress.com.

However if you're on WordPress.org, you have the pick of the providers. They all have a plugin which you can use to get mailing list signups on your website. Which is one of the reasons for choosing a self-hosted WordPress site.

Let's find out a bit more about them.

NEWSLETTER PROVIDERS

There are plenty of newsletter providers. These are some of the ones that have plugins for WordPress.org:

- MailChimp.
- MailerLite.
- ConvertKit.
- Constant Contact.
- AWeber.

This book isn't about newsletters (if you want the ultimate guide to those, I recommend the book *Newsletter Ninja* by Tammi Labrecque), so I'm not going to spend time analyzing the different providers and telling you which one to choose.

For many authors, MailChimp is the most suitable provider. This is for a number of reasons:

- It's the easiest to integrate with other services such as WordPress.com and Facebook ads.
- It's got a user-friendly interface which isn't too complicated.
- Until you have 2,000 readers on your list, it's (sort of) free.
- Its automation features, while not as powerful as some of the other providers, are plenty good enough for an author mailing list.

I use MailChimp for some of my mailing lists (I have three), because of the free thing and also because I can hook it up to Facebook and run ads designed to add people to my list, without having to redirect people to my site. If you want to learn how to do this, I can recommend Mark Dawson's excellent course on list-building for authors at wp4writers.com/dawson.

Once you hit 2,000 subscribers, you'll have to start paying for the privilege of running your mailing list. So if you think this will happen quickly, it pays to look at some of the other providers too. If your list is large or your automation needs are complex, one of those may be the most appropriate.

But at the time of writing, things have recently become more complicated. MailChimp have changed their terms, meaning many authors have to pay more (learn more at wp4writers.com/mailchimp-changes). Many authors are switching to alternative providers, my favorite of which is MailerLite.

In this section of the book, I'm going to focus on MailChimp, because it's the most popular platform among authors, and on MailerLite, because that's the most user-friendly alternative in my opinion. I use MailerLite for one of my lists and will likely migrate the others to it over time.

MailChimp has its benefits: it's the only platform you can link to WordPress.com and to Facebook ads, and it is free up to a point. But MailerLite has a better user interface, a plugin for WordPress.org, and a clearly defined forever-free plan for people with less than 1,000 subscribers on their list.

It's up to you which you choose: but those are the two I'll be looking at here.

In the next two chapters, I'll show you how to integrate your mailing list and your website. The first chapter will look at WordPress.com and the second at WordPress.org. So pick the one for you, and read on.

USING WORDPRESS.COM FOR NEWSLETTER SIGNUPS

Until quite recently, it wasn't possible to collect newsletter subscribers from your WordPress.com site and send them to your mailing list provider without either pasting some code into your site or copying the data manually.

Neither of those are things you want to send your time doing. So when WordPress added MailChimp integration, I did a little dance of joy. So convenient that they did it just in time for this book! (Did they know?)

However, at the time of writing, MailChimp have just changed their terms of service, meaning that you could end up having to pay for MailChimp before you reach 2,000 active subscribers. Lots of authors rightly think this is unfair and are switching providers.

The alternative provider I would recommend (because they're free for up to 1,000 subscribers, and have no plans to change that) is MailerLite. However, you can't link your WordPress.com site directly to them, so you need to use a workaround.

Which you use is up to you: MailChimp is simpler, but could cost you more in the long run. So in this chapter, I'll show you how to use both.

CREATING A SIGNUP PAGE

The first step is to create a page where people will sign up, which is the same whichever provider you're using.

Create a new static page and give it a name. This might be something like 'newsletter' or 'book club', or you might name it after the resource you're giving people as a thank you for joining your list.

Add some text to the page with information about what people will get in return for their email address. I like to add a photo of the book that I'm giving away. This is known as a Reader Magnet.

Reader Magnet? What's that?

A reader magnet is a freebie that you give people in return for their email address. This might be a free book, story or novella, or something else. For my nonfiction, I give away a short book, while for my fiction I give away a story collection.

If you don't give anything away, you're less likely to get people signing up. Once you've identified what your reader magnet will be, make sure you tell people about it in the back matter of your books and give them a link to get their hands on it.

You'll also need to consider how you will deliver the reader magnet to readers. The most popular method is via BookFunnel. You can find out more about this at wp4writers.com/bookfunnel.

Once you've added some text to your page, it's time to add the signup form or link.

LINKING WORDPRESS.COM AND MAILCHIMP

If you're using MailChimp, you need to link your WordPress.com and MailChimp accounts.

Note: if you're using WordPress.org with the Jetpack plugin you can also link your site to MailChimp this way, and you won't need to install an extra plugin.

In the WordPress dashboard, go to **Tools > Marketing** and click on the **Connections** tab.

Scroll down until you see the **MailChimp** option.

Image 29-1 Accessing MailChimp in WordPress.com

If you already have a MailChimp account, click the **Connect** button. If you don't, click **Sign up** and you will be taken through the process of signing up to MailChimp as well as connecting it to WordPress.com.

You will then be prompted for your MailChimp username and password. Type these in and click the **Log in** button (if you're also signing up, follow the instructions given first).

Once you've done that, you'll need to select the mailing list that you're going to be linking to. I've got three so I have to tell Word-Press which one I want to connect.

Image 29-2 Selecting a mailing list

Once you've done that, it's time to create your signup page.

ADDING A MAILCHIMP SIGNUP FORM

To add a signup form to your page, you use the MailChimp block.

Click the **+** icon to add a new block and select the **MailChimp** block. This will add a field for the reader's email address and some text about how their data will be used. This text is designed to comply with data regulations so don't remove it—but you may want to tweak it a little to reflect your writing style. You can also change the text in the button.

On the right-hand side of the screen, in the **Blocks** pane, you can edit elements such as the button and text color and the text people will see after successfully signing up.

Take some time to tweak the settings and make it work for you and your readers. This is one of the most important blocks in your site so it's important to get it right.

Once you're happy with it, click the **Publish** button, go through the normal pre-publish checks, and hit **Publish** again. You can also preview it before publishing.

If your theme includes a full-width page template, it makes sense to use that as it minimizes distractions. You want to have as few links as possible in that page other than the sign-up link.

Here's how mine is looking:

Image 29-3 Editing the newsletter signup page

Congratulations! You now have a newsletter sign-up page.

LINKING WORDPRESS.COM AND MAILERLITE

If you want to link your WordPress.com site to a MailerLite account, you'll need to use a workaround. MailerLite doesn't have a direct integration with WordPress.com (unless you're on an expensive plan that lets you install plugins, which I wouldn't recommend) but that doesn't mean you can't gather signups on your WordPress.com site.

Start by creating an account with MailerLite and setting up a list with the relevant fields. Create your welcome sequence and test it.

Instead of gathering addresses in your website, you'll use a landing page on the MailerLite site. Follow their instructions (wp4writers.com/ml-landing) to set one up that collects the data you need and fits with your brand.

Now go back to your signup page in your WordPress.com site. Add a Button block and have it link to your landing page in MailerLite.

This way, you're using MailerLite's landing page, but the link you use in your books' back matter and everywhere else will be to your site. Which means it's future-proofed: if you ever change mailing list providers in the future, you won't need to change that link.

ADDING A HOME PAGE BANNER LINKING TO YOUR SIGNUP PAGE

Now that you have your signup page, you want to make it as easy as possible for people to find it. With a free WordPress.com account, there aren't any themes that include a clickable banner, but you can fake this.

First, visit your landing page (the signup page) in your site. Copy the URL for this page (you'll find it in your browser at the top).

In the admin screen, open your home page. At the very top of the page, add an image block. Make sure this image is wide and includes text encouraging people to grab their copy of your reader magnet. You can see the image I use in my fiction site below.

Image 29-4 The banner image for my fiction site

After adding the image, make sure the **Block** pane is open on the right-hand side of the editing screen, and scroll down to the **Link Settings** section. Click on the **Link to** dropdown list and select **Custom URL**. In the field that appears, paste in the URL of your landing page, that you already copied.

Save your home page as a draft and preview it (it's important to do this to make sure it works before going live). If it looks good and the link works, publish it.

You now have a banner in your home page linking to your signup page.

ADDING A WIDGET LINKING TO YOUR SIGNUP PAGE

As well as a banner in the home page, it's a good idea to have a link to your signup page appearing everywhere on your site. You don't want a dirty great banner on every page as that will start to annoy people, but you can add a widget to your sidebar.

In the WordPress.com admin, go to **Design > Customize** and select **Widgets**.

Select the widget area you want to add the link to (I recommend using the sidebar widget area and placing this widget at the top). Click the **Add a Widget** button.

Scroll down and select the **Text** widget. You can now type your text into the widget and add an image too, as well as the all-important link.

The widget you're creating will be previewed on the right of the screen. When you're happy with it, click **Publish** and it'll be saved.

*Note: Whenever you make a change using the Customizer, always click **Publish**, or your changes won't be saved.*

Well done! You now have a widget encouraging people to sign up for your mailing list, and taking them to the signup page.

INSTALLING AND CONFIGURING A MAILING LIST PLUGIN

So. You're a WordPress.org user (well done you) and you skipped the last chapter. You want to know how to link your self-hosted WordPress site with your mailing list.

The good news is that it's incredibly easy, thanks to the existence of plugins for all the major mailing list providers.

You'll find that WordPress has free plugins for all of the providers listed below, and more:

- MailChimp
- MailerLite
- ConvertKit
- Constant Contact
- AWeber

But in this book, I'm going to show you how to do it with Mail-Chimp and with MailerLite. Let's start with MailChimp.

WHY MAILCHIMP?

As I already mentioned a couple of chapters back, in the past, I've used MailChimp for my mailing list.

The main reason I chose it is because of the ease of linking it to my Facebook list-building ads. At the time of writing, it's the only mailing list provider that lets you directly link to Facebook. This means that if you run ads to get people to sign up to your mailing list, it'll collect the addresses and put them straight into your list in MailChimp. If you're using another provider, you'll have to copy the data across yourself. I don't want to do that, as I want people who respond to one of my ads to receive their welcome email immediately.

So that's why I use MailChimp for at least one of my mailing lists. And if you're new to creating an author website and setting up a mailing list, it's the one I recommend for you. This is because it's easy to learn, not over-complicated, and—importantly—it's free for the first 2,000 subscribers.

However—and this is quite a big caveat—at the time of writing, MailChimp recently changed their terms, meaning that for a lot of authors, running a MailChimp list will be more expensive, and that the free plan will end before you have 2,000 subscribers (they count people who've unsubscribed, which seems pretty unfair). So I've been migrating some of my mailing lists to MailerLite. Which is why I'm including MailerLite in this chapter as well.

For many authors, MailChimp will still be appropriate, because of those integrations or maybe because you've already got a Mail-Chimp account and aren't ready to switch. So first I'm going to show you how to hook your WordPress.org website up to Mail-Chimp, using the MailChimp plugin.

> *Note: If you're using the Jetpack plugin and you'd rather not install an extra plugin, you can link MailChimp to your website in the same way you would for WordPress.com. See the previous chapter for details.*

Happy with that? Good. Let's go.

INSTALLING THE MAILCHIMP PLUGIN

First, you'll need to install the MailChimp plugin to be able to connect your website to your mailing list.

In your WordPress dashboard, go to **Plugins > Add New**. Type *mailchimp* into the search box and you'll see the MailChimp plugin.

Click the **Install** button. WordPress will install the plugin and the button will change to an **Activate** button. Click it again to activate the plugin.

That's step one done. Easy so far, huh?

LINKING THE PLUGIN TO YOUR MAILING LIST

Now you need to get your site to talk to your mailing list, via the plugin settings.

A new item will have appeared in your admin menu, called **MailChimp for WP**. Click on that to see the MailChimp settings screen:

You are here: Mailchimp for WordPress

Mailchimp for WordPress: API Settings

Status   CONNECTED

API Key   *******************3bce912e7b5acc-us2

The API key for connecting with your Mailchimp account. Get your API key here.

Save Changes

Your Mailchimp Account

The table below shows your Mailchimp lists and their details. If you just applied changes to your Mailchimp lists, please use the following button to renew the cached lists configuration.

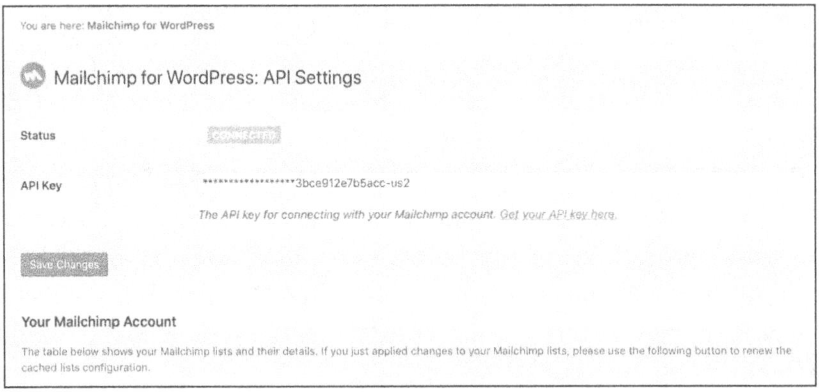

Image 30-1 The MailChimp Settings screen

You'll need to provide your API key from MailChimp to get the plugin to work. To do that, click the link in the settings screen. It will take you to your MailChimp account. Log in to that if you're not already logged in, and you'll see the **API Keys** screen.

Copy the API key from that screen and paste it into the **API Key** field back in the plugin settings screen in WordPress. Click the **Save Changes** button.

A list of your mailing lists will now appear at the bottom of the settings screen (you may need to scroll down). Your MailChimp account is now linked to your website. Yay!

CREATING THE MAILCHIMP FORM

You're not done yet. Now you need to add the form which people will use to sign up to your mailing list. You do this before creating the page where it will live.

Still in the WordPress admin screens, go to **MailChimp for WP > Form**. Here's where you set up the form. If you want multiple forms or you want to add people to groups within your lists, you'll need the premium MailChimp plugin: there's a link to that on the right-hand side of the screen. But for most authors, the free version will suffice.

Type in what you want the form to be called and select the list it will link to.

Click the **Add New Form** button and your form will be saved.

If you want to edit your form or change which list it links to, you can do this via the **Settings** tab on the **Form** page. You can also add extra fields via the **Fields** tab. Beware editing the code directly: it's safest just to use the buttons.

You can also edit any messages using the **Messages** tab. Edit the confirmation message to let people know what to expect from your mailing list and to reassure them that you won't share their email or spam them.

ADDING THE MAILCHIMP FORM TO YOUR SIGNUP PAGE

You add your form to your page with the block provided by the plugin.

Start by creating a new static page. Add some text to this to encourage people to sign up or tell them something about your reader magnet. You might also add a photo of your reader magnet.

Now add a new block by clicking the **+** icon, then select **Widgets > MailChimp for WordPress Form**. A form will be added to your page.

There isn't much you can do to customize the form: it will take its styling from your theme. If you'd rather customize the button, use the Jetpack plugin instead and follow the instructions in the previous chapter.

Once you're happy with your form, you can publish your post and then link to it from your home page banner and from a widget in the sidebar.

INSTALLING THE MAILERLITE PLUGIN

So you've decided you want to use a mailing list provider that doesn't mess its users around by suddenly changing its terms and prices. Shrewd move. Here's how to link your site to MailerLite.

To install the MailerLite plugin, go to **Plugins > Add New**. Find the MailerLite plugin by typing *mailerlite* into the search box. A plugin called **Official MailerLite Signup Forms** (snappy) will appear. Install and activate that.

LINKING YOUR MAILERLITE ACCOUNT TO YOUR WEBSITE

First you'll need to find your API key. In your MailerLite dashboard, click on the **Integrations** link in the admin menu at the top right of the screen. In the screen that appears, click the **Developer API** button. You'll find your API key listed: copy it.

Now back in WordPress, go to **MailerLite > Settings** and copy in your API key. Click the **Save this key** button. This will link your site to MailerLite.

CREATING A FORM FOR MAILERLITE SIGNUPS

Now to create a form you can use for signups. Still in WordPress, go to **MailerLite > Signup forms** and click the **Add new** button.

Select **Custom signup form** and click the **Create form** button. Select the mailing list this form will apply to and click the **Create form** button.

You'll be taken to the screen for editing and creating your form. Add the fields you need and configure the notification and confirmation messages. I just have one field: email address. The more fields you add, the less people will sign up. Name your form and then when you're happy with it, save it.

ADDING THE MAILERLITE FORM TO YOUR SIGNUP PAGE

Now it's time to create your signup page and add the form to it. Create a static page in the normal way. If your theme has a full-width page template, use that to minimise distractions.

Add some text and an image of your reader magnet, then create a new block and select the **MailerLite sign up form** block type. Select the form you just created and publish your signup page.

That's it! You now have a page where people can directly sign up to your MailerLite mailing list.

ADDING A SIGNUP WIDGET

You have two choices when it comes to adding a mailing list widget to your sidebar: you can either add a text widget that links to your signup page, or you can add a MailChimp or MailerLite widget which lets people sign up right from the widget.

Personally, I prefer to take people to my signup page, as I can tell them more about my reader magnet. But if you'd like to allow signups right in the widget, you can use the widget provided with your mailing list plugin to do this.

Note: For instructions on adding a text widget linking to your signup page, see the previous chapter.

Go to **Appearance > Widgets** to see the widget editing screen (or open the Customizer and select **Widgets**). Which widget areas you have available to you will depend on your theme, but most themes will have a sidebar, which is the most common place to put this widget.

Find the **MailChimp Sign-Up Form** or **MailerLite Sign-Up Form** widget in the list on the left and drag it over to the widget area where you want it to appear. Edit the title of the widget—this is what people will see. Select which form you want to display if you've created more than one.

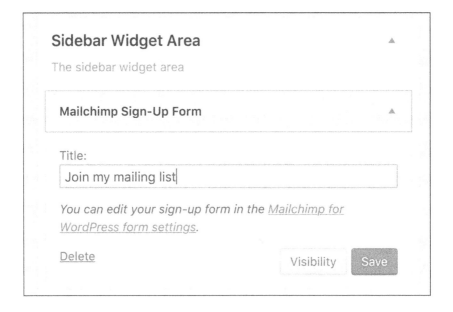

Image 30-2 Creating the MailChimp widget

Now save that and check your site. You should see a shiny new mailing list signup in your sidebar.

That's it! People can now sign up to your mailing list from every page in your site.

LINKING TO YOUR SIGNUP PAGE FROM THE HOME PAGE BANNER

A bold home page banner that encourages people to click through to your signup page is a good idea. You don't want anyone missing that opportunity, after all.

You can do this in one of two ways:

- If your theme includes a home page banner that can be used as a link, upload your banner to that and add the link to your signup page. You get that link by visiting your signup page and copying the URL from the top of the browser window.
- If your theme doesn't include a banner image that can be used as a clickable link, create one by uploading a suitable image to your home page's content. You can find out how to do this in the previous chapter.

NINJA TRICK

There is research that shows that if people have to click an extra link before providing their email address, then they'll be more likely to complete the form and give their email address. Something to do with that extra click making them feel more invested in the process —odd, I know.

To take advantage of this, you can add an extra page to your site which people will go through when signing up for your mailing list. This is called a landing page.

To do this, follow these steps:

1. Connect to MailChimp or MailerLite and create your signup page as described above. Leave out the detailed information about your reader magnet.
2. Create another static page (your landing page) with information about your reader magnet. Below that, add a button using the **Button** block. Edit the text in the

button to read 'get my copy' or something similar, and tweak the colors so they're consistent with your signup page. The button should link to the signup page.

3. When you add a banner and/or a text widget, make sure these link to the landing page. People will click though to that, read about your reader magnet, be intrigued enough to click the button, then go to the signup page.

Try adding this extra step and see if it makes a difference. And if you want to see it in action, go to my landing page at rachelmcwrites.com/blueprint. (See what I did there?)

VII

KER-CHING! SELLING BOOKS
FROM YOUR WEBSITE

SELLING BOOKS FROM YOUR SITE

THIS IS advanced territory we're getting into here.

Most authors will never sell books directly from their website. They'll be happy to take advantage of the platforms provided by the online book retailers (and to sell in physical bookstores), and would rather save themselves the time and hassle.

If that's you, I get it. There are real benefits to selling books in the places designed to sell books.

But selling books direct also has its benefits. Read on to find out if it might be worth considering.

WHY SELL BOOKS ON YOUR WEBSITE?

Let's start by looking at some of the reasons you might choose to sell books on your website.

- You'll earn 100% of the sale value of the book (minus a small fee if you use a payment facility such as PayPal).
- You can sell your books at a lower price because of not having to pay royalties.

- If you can buy paperbacks at a reduced author rate, you can sell signed copies direct to fans.
- You have total control.

WHEN NOT TO SELL BOOKS ON YOUR WEBSITE

OK, so let's look at some of the reasons you might not sell books on your website.

- If you're selling physical books, you'll have to arrange postage (make sure you charge for this and factor in international shipping where relevant).
- You'll lose the ranking benefit that you get for sales on the online bookstores.
- Your books will be harder to find than on Amazon and the other big bookstores.
- You'll have to find a way of delivering e-books securely (BookFunnel is my favorite option as it has a way of ensuring each link is only used once, but you could do this right from WordPress).

There are also reasons why some authors won't be able to sell their books direct. This isn't about the pros and cons, it's about not being permitted.

- If you're with a publishing house you won't own the rights to your books and so can't sell them direct. Some publishers are OK with authors selling a limited number of signed paperbacks—you'll need to check. But you definitely won't be able to sell e-books for which you don't own the rights.
- If your e-books are enrolled in KDP Select (i.e. they're available via Kindle Unlimited), Amazon's exclusivity requirement means you won't be allowed to sell them direct.(You can still sell your paperbacks though.)

If you're with a publishing house and you're in doubt, I suggest checking with them. If you're an indie, the only restriction is KDP Select exclusivity.

USING WOOCOMMERCE TO SELL BOOKS

WooCommerce is the most popular e-commerce platform available, and it can be installed for free with a self-hosted WordPress site.

It's also available with WordPress.com, but you'll have to pay for one of the higher paid plans. If you plan to sell using WooCommerce, I think you'd have to be mad to do this with WordPress.com, as it'll cost you more and offer you less flexibility. Go for self-hosted WordPress instead.

To use WooCommerce to sell your books, you'll need a few things:

- An account with PayPal, Stripe or similar to take payments.
- The WooCommerce plugin, which you can install for free via the Plugins screen.
- A theme that's compatible with WooCommerce. Most themes work just fine with WooCommerce, although if you do plan to sell online, this'll be something you should look for when you choose the theme for your site (include *woocommerce* in your keywords when searching for a theme via the Themes screen).
- Photos of your books (the covers, of course), and anything else you plan to sell.
- The means to ship products. For digital downloads, you can set this up via WooCommerce or BookFunnel in a way that ensures each download link can only be used once. For physical books, you'll need to take payment for postage and send books out yourself.
- The time to manage orders if you're selling physical books. For e-books, the process will happen

automatically and you won't need to do anything unless there's a problem.

Selling via WooCommerce is easier than you might think and can make you some extra money from your books. But it takes time to set up properly, so I recommend you check out the WooCommerce documentation at wp4writers.com/woocommerce.

VIII

ENGAGING WITH YOUR READERS

BELOW THE LINE: COMMENTS

I'VE ALREADY TALKED about your newsletter and how it's a great way to engage with your readers. Using your newsletter, you can send readers updates on your work and start a dialogue by asking them questions in every email, encouraging them to reply and give you feedback or ask you more.

But there are other ways to engage with your readers via your website, and one of them is the commenting system.

WHAT DO COMMENTS DO?

Comments give visitors to your website the opportunity to give feedback on your content or ask questions about it.

If you're used to the 'below the line' (BTL) section on some of the more notorious websites, you might be wary of enabling comments in your author site. Why encourage the trolls?

But most trolls aren't interested in leaving comments on your website. Instead, you're far more likely to get comments from readers who liked your posts or want to know more about your books.

If you don't enable comments in your site, you're missing out on an opportunity to engage with readers, one that you have more control over than you do your social media channels.

ACTIVATING COMMENTS

Firstly, you'll need to ensure comments are activated for your site.

- In WordPress.com, go to **Manage > Settings** and click on the **Discussion** tab.
- In self-hosted WordPress, go to **Settings > Discussion**.

Here you can toggle comments and pingbacks on or off. Leave them all on.

Pingbacks? What are they, games of ping pong?

Pingbacks are when someone links to your site from another site and the link is shown in the comments on your site. A snippet of text will also be shown displaying the text used with the link.

If you turn pingbacks off, people will still be able to link to your site—but you won't know about it. Not every link will be picked up by pingbacks: it's just links from other blogs, not from social media, for example.

You can also edit the text at the top of the comments section (the default is *Leave a Reply*) and turn on other comment settings designed to keep out trolls and enhance security. The defaults work fine for me.

I'm not going to go through all the comment settings here, but do advise you to take some time to work through them and check that they're configured the way you want them. It's important to leave on notifications when you get comments, so that you can reply to them.

But what if you're worried about spam? There's a plugin for that.

BANISHING COMMENT SPAM WITH AKISMET

Although it's unlikely that your website will attract trolls, the chances are that it will attract spammers. This is because most spam is automated. As soon as a new website pops up, the spambots will target it, hurling adverts for Viagra and other things you don't want at your comments section.

There is an easy way to stop this, and it's called Akismet.

If you're on WordPress.com, you already have Akismet as part of your site. It will work to banish spammy comments and trash them without you ever knowing about them. I've checked the comments that Akismet has blocked from my sites and can testify that it is accurate and reliable: it gets rid of almost all spammy comments and doesn't block the genuine ones. It's able to do this because it's installed on millions of websites worldwide and can learn from the data it gathers from them all.

If you're on WordPress.org, you'll need to either add Jetpack or set up the Akismet plugin. This normally comes bundled with WordPress, although some hosting providers don't include it with their one-click install. If you don't see it listed in your Plugins screen, just install it as you would any plugin and activate it.

Once you've activated the plugin, you'll see a big button at the top of the Plugins screen to set up your Akismet account. Click on it. If you can't see it, go to **Settings > Akismet anti-spam** and click the **Get your API key** button.

This will take you to the Akismet website. Click on the button to activate Akismet. Next you can either sign up for Akismet with your WordPress.com account if you have one, or create one.

Note: If you have the Jetpack plugin, use the WordPress.com account created when you set that up. Similarly, if you install Jetpack after this, use the account set up for Akismet when you're signing up for that.

You then have the option to choose the account level you want. Choose **Personal**. This gives you the option to pay what you want. Bearing in mind that Akismet (and WordPress.com) is run by a multi-million-dollar company that's not short of cash, you might choose to sign up for free. Use the slider on the right-hand side of the next screen to select **$0/year** and type your name and site name on the left. Check all the checkboxes and click the button to continue.

You'll then be presented with your API key, but you can also click a link to activate your site. Do it, and you're all set. If that link doesn't work, copy the API key then go back to the Akismet settings screen in your site and paste it in there.

You can then tweak your Akismet settings, opting to put the really spammy stuff (spam that would do Monty Python proud, a reference you'll probably only get if you're British, sorry!) into the trash and not the spam folder. Or if you want to experience the delight of reading your spammy comments, leave it as it is, going to the spam folder. Click **Save Changes** and you're done.

Now you won't see spammy comments popping up under your posts. And you won't have to do anything more to make it happen.

ENHANCING COMMENTS: SOCIAL MEDIA INTEGRATION AND MORE

If you're on WordPress.com, you have access to an enhanced commenting form that lets people sign in via Facebook or other social media in order to post a comment. It also lets them use their WordPress.com account if they have one.

This will make it easier for people to comment, and encourage more comments.

On WordPress.org, the default comments form is a little sparser. People have to provide their name and email address in order to leave a comment. But with the Jetpack plugin, you can add the WordPress.com comments form to your self-hosted site.

To activate the enhanced comments form, go to **Jetpack > Settings** and select the **Discussion** tab. Toggle the option to **Use**

WordPress.com, Facebook, Twitter etc. to comment to on. It'll automatically start working on your site.

GET PEOPLE TALKING: ENCOURAGING COMMENTS

So: you've got comments enabled on your site, you've eliminated spam, and you're waiting for those avid readers to leave hundreds of comments.

Err, it doesn't happen quite like that.

Comments will only start to take off when your site starts to take off, and even then, you'll have to put some effort into it.

Here are some tips to encourage more comments:

- Drive more traffic to your site with SEO and social sharing.
- Write engaging, relevant content that makes people want to comment.
- Be deliberately provocative. Beware: this can attract the trolls. Keep it relevant and remember if you get a comment you don't like, you can delete it. This is your site, not Mark Zuckerberg's.
- Ask questions. At the end of your posts (and even better, at the beginning too), ask people for their opinions/advice/suggestions. The questions that can be most successful at getting comments are the ones that encourage people to show off. Ask a question that gives people the opportunity to show how clever or accomplished they are and your chances of getting comments will grow.

Don't worry too much if you don't get many comments, or if it's a while until they start coming. I know of bloggers who are close to burnout because of the time they have to spend managing comments—it's not always a good thing, even if the comments are positive!

BE RESPONSIVE: RESPONDING TO COMMENTS

But when you do get comments, it's a good idea to reply to them.

You'll get an email when you get a new comment. Follow it up: mark the comment as not spam (assuming it isn't spam), otherwise it won't be published. Then reply to it. WordPress lets you do this either on the post itself or in the Comments section of the admin screens.

If a reader has taken the time to contact you via the comments, they'll be over the moon if you reply. To them, you're a writer: a minor celebrity. It'll make them more of a fan and more likely to buy more of your books and recommend you to their friends. Don't pass it up.

THE HOLY GRAIL: WHEN READERS TALK TO EACH OTHER ABOUT YOUR BOOKS

The best scenario is when you don't even need to reply to your own comments, and that's because your readers are doing it for you.

Sometimes, you'll write a post that gets people engaged in a discussion among themselves. They'll reply to each other's posts and start a debate.

If this happens, resist the temptation to jump in. Instead, watch the discussion and wait until there's a lull. Then, instead of answering the original question, pose more questions. Fuel that debate.

This will build a community around your work: something every author craves.

WHEN COMMENTS GO WRONG

There will be times when spammy comments get through the Akismet filter, or a troll writes something you don't like in the comments.

If this happens, don't fret. It's your site. Just spam or delete the comment and move on.

If you spam the comment, the commenter will be barred from making more comments. Think carefully before doing this: if this person has commented before, and the comments have been positive, they could be a fan with a valid opinion.

And if someone leaves a negative review of your work (either a post or a book), you can choose to delete it, or to leave it there and wait for other commenters to disagree. You never know, it may harden their support for you!

But the important thing to remember is that this is your site, your content: if a comment isn't going to help you attract readers and sell books, you can remove it.

33

THE WORDPRESS.COM COMMUNITY

As well as comments, you also have access to engagement via the WordPress.com community.

This is the community of everyone with a WordPress.com account. So that'll include everyone with a WordPress.com site, everyone with the Jetpack plugin, everyone using Akismet to banish comment spam, and everyone who's set up an account so they can follow a blog they like. That's a lot of people.

If you have any of these things, there is a real benefit to engaging with the WordPress.com community.

ENCOURAGING FOLLOWS

You can encourage people to follow your site by adding a Follow widget to your sidebar.

In WordPress.com, go to **Design > Customize** and select **Widgets**. Find the **Follow** widget. Add that to your sidebar (I'd recommend putting it near the widget taking people to your newsletter signup page) and edit the text if you want.

In WordPress.org, go to **Appearance > Customize** and Select **Widgets** or go to the Widgets screen via **Appearance >**

Widgets. Select the **Blog Subscription (Jetpack)** widget and add that to your widget area.

When people follow your site, they'll receive an email every time you add a new post—without you having to lift a finger.

You can find out who's following your site in the WordPress.com admin. If you're using Jetpack, you'll have to sign into this using the WordPress.com account you created when you installed Jetpack.

Go to **Manage > People** and select the **Followers** tab. You'll see a list of all the people following your site. You can click on their names to see their sites and follow them back if you want.

FOLLOWING OTHER BLOGGERS

It's a good idea to become engaged in the community of bloggers by following other WordPress.com (or Jetpack-enabled) sites.

Go to the WordPress.com dashboard and click the **Reader** link at the top of the screen. Click on **Discover** to discover other blogs. You can search for individual bloggers and for topics you're interested in.

Once you've followed people, you'll get an email when they post an update. You can also view their updates in WordPress.com.

In the WordPress.com dashboard, click on **My Likes** to see all the sites you're following, with their latest updates. Here you can see the latest updates from the blogs you're following and choose whether to receive notifications from each of them or not.

Find other authors or people who blog about the topics you write about. Join in the discussion and make contact with them; you could form some valuable connections.

IX

SITE HOUSEKEEPING

3 4

A CLEAN AND TIDY WEBSITE

Your site is up and running and you've started posting content.

But your job isn't done yet (sorry). You still have to maintain the site and keep it clean and tidy. In this section of the book, I'll give you some tips on site housekeeping. I'll include keeping your site secure and backed up, and making sure the software is up to date.

Much of this is already done for you with WordPress.com, and can be automated in WordPress.org. Read on and find out how.

WHY KEEP YOUR SITE IN ORDER?

There are a number of good reasons to keep your site tidy:

- Keeping your themes and plugins updated, as well as WordPress itself, will minimize any security risks.
- Keeping your site backed up will ensure that if there's a problem, you can fix it.
- Making your site clean and fast will enhance your search engine rankings.

WHAT HAPPENS WHEN YOU LET THINGS SLIDE

Remember that story I told way back in Chapter 15 about my website being hacked when I was on a camping holiday?

That happened because I hadn't run an update on my site.

In those days, automatic updates were less reliable and I chose not to install a plugin which would enable them. (Things are a bit different now, and minor updates will be done for you automatically.) I was on holiday, and had been busy clearing my to-do list before going away. Which meant I hadn't updated my site.

The update I'd missed had probably included a security patch, one that the hackers exploited to access my site.

So it's really important to keep your site up to date, for security reasons.

Looking after your site will also prevent you slipping in the search rankings and annoying visitors with a site that's slower to load than it should be.

So do it, right?

ESTABLISHING A ROUTINE

Keeping your site up to date will only happen if you have a routine. You can also automate a lot of the processes.

In WordPress.com, you don't need to worry about backups, updates or security. It's all handled for you.

But with WordPress.org, you can install plugins that will help you with this, and will do a lot of the spring cleaning while you're busy doing something else (writing, maybe?).

Backups, updates and performance can all be automated. But you'll need to set them up first. And it's good practice to get into a routine of checking your site over once a month, just to be sure everything is running smoothly.

Read on and find out how to get everything ticking along nicely.

KEEPING YOUR SITE BACKED UP

I'M DELIBERATELY INCLUDING backups first.

And that's because if you don't back up your site, you could lose it.

I mean that. It's been known for hosting providers to lose a site completely, and without a backup, you could be in deep doo-doo.

THE IMPORTANCE OF BACKUPS

Way back when I first started with WordPress, I hosted my client sites with a small hosting provider that I think was run from someone's bedroom.

One Monday morning, I woke to an email from one of my clients saying his site had gone down. I checked my other clients' sites and they were all down too.

I emailed all my clients to warn them and let them know that I was looking into it, then raised a support ticket with my hosting provider...

...who had been moving data from one server to another...

...and had lost everything.

Everything. They didn't have a backup, they didn't have access to my sites. They were gone.

Disaster!

Luckily, I kept my own backups. But with every single client site lost, it took some time to restore them all from those backups, ending with my own.

I lost a lot of time. I switched my hosting to a company with an uptime guarantee (meaning they give you a refund if your site goes down) and started the process of transferring all the domain names to the new provider and getting all the sites working again.

It was horrible, but it would have been far, far worse if I hadn't been keeping backups. I had backup files I could use to restore every client site I managed, which saved my skin.

That's why it's important to keep backups.

WHY RESTORING IS MORE IMPORTANT THAN BACKING UP

When people choose a backup plugin, they often go for one that makes it easy to backup their site.

But I think you should choose one that makes it easy to *restore* your site.

Why? Because your site never goes down when you want it to. If it does ever happen to you (and I hope it doesn't: I've managed upwards of 20 sites for almost ten years and have had it happen only twice), you'll be panicking.

You want a restore process that is so easy your grandma could do it for you (with apologies to all those tech-savvy grandmas out there).

CHOOSING A BACKUP PLUGIN

The first thing to do is choose your backup plugin. You have three options:

- Get a premium WordPress.com account via the Jetpack plugin and use that.
- Install a free plugin.
- Pay for a premium plugin.

I haven't used the premium backup option with Jetpack but I have no doubt as to its reliability and ease of use. But it's expensive.

If you go with a free plugin, I recommend UpdraftPlus, which I'll be focusing on in the rest of this chapter.

And if you go for a premium plugin, the best in my opinion are Updraft Plus Premium and Snapshot Pro.

The premium plugins have a slightly more intuitive user interface and make the process of restoring your site just that bit easier. For extra peace of mind, it may be worth investing in one of these. But if you want to stick with free (which I'm encouraging throughout this book), then UpdraftPlus is reliable and lets you save your backups to an external service like Dropbox or Google Drive, which is more reliable than saving it on your website server.

WHERE SHOULD YOU STORE YOUR BACKUPS?

…Which brings me to backup storage.

There's a very good reason why you shouldn't keep your backups on the same server where your website is hosted. Or at least, why you shouldn't exclusively keep them there. It's fine to keep one copy there and one elsewhere.

If your server goes down, or your hosting provider goes belly-up, you want to have access to your backups. So you need them to be stored somewhere independently of your website.

Here are your backup storage options:

- On your computer. This way, you have the plugin send backups to you by email and then you save them to your computer. This is OK but relies on you remembering to save the files every time and can take up a lot of space on your computer. And once your site reaches a certain size, the files will be too large to send by email.

- On Dropbox. Dropbox is the most popular cloud storage service and is free for up to 5GB of space. As long as you delete old backups periodically, this will do the job. If you want to keep more backups, you may have to sign up for a premium plan.
- On Google Drive. If you have a Google account, you already have access to this. It's free for up to 15GB (three times as much as with Dropbox) and if you do need more space, you can get up to 130GB for less than a couple of bucks a month.

Unless you're already using Dropbox, I'd recommend using Google Drive. If you don't already have a Google account, you can set one up and get access to Google Drive at wp4writers.com/googledrive.

The plugin will give you alternative storage options, but they're less user-friendly than these so don't worry about them.

KEEP YOUR SITE BACKED UP WHILE YOU SLEEP

OK, so now you know why backups are important and where you should store them.

It's time to set up backups and have them run automatically.

Start off my installing the UpdraftPlus plugin in the normal way and activating it.

> *Note: The process for any backup plugin is very similar. So if you choose to use a premium plugin, keep reading and tweak as necessary.*

Go to **Settings > UpdraftPlus Backups**. Click on the **Settings** tab.

First, you need to specify how often you want to run a backup. This should coincide with the frequency with which you intend to add new content. If you're writing new posts weekly, choose **Weekly**; if you're updating more often, choose **Daily**.

You can also choose how many backups will be kept. This is how many backups will be kept on the server, not on your remote storage (e.g. Google Drive), as that is unlimited.

Then choose your remote storage provider. There are quite a few: select **Google Drive** (or **Dropbox** if you're using that).

Ignore the next few options, where you choose the files and database tables to back up—leave this on the default settings.

Check the **Email** box if you want to have an email report sent to you every time the site is backed up (useful in case anything goes wrong), and then click the **Save Changes** button.

You'll then see a popup with a link to authorize your remote storage. Click on it.

Sign in to your Google account and click the **Allow** button to allow the plugin to send files to Google Drive. You'll then be shown another screen with a button to go back to your site. Click it.

And that's it! Your site will now be automatically be backed up for you on a regular basis.

What if I want to run a backup right now?

It's a good idea to do this when you first install the plugin, so you're not waiting for the next automatic backup and you know you have one right now.

To run a manual backup, go to **Settings > UpdraftPlus Backups** (or click the **Backup/Restore** tab if you're already in the plugin settings). Click the big button that says **Backup Now**. Leave all the checkboxes on the popup as they are and click **Backup** again. A backup will run immediately.

WHEN THINGS GO WRONG: RESTORING YOUR SITE

This is the important bit. Backing up your site is no good unless you can restore it again when there's a problem.

If you discover that your site's been hacked or isn't working, start by asking yourself when it was last working. When did you last visit it and not have any problems?

Let's say that was two days ago. That means your best backup to restore from is one from more than two days ago.

This is why it's useful to keep multiple backups. I like to keep a week's worth on sites I back up daily, and a month's worth on sites I back up weekly.

So, your site has crashed or been hacked. Don't panic. Just follow these steps.

1. Go to **Settings > UpdraftPlus Backups**.
2. Scroll down to the **Existing Backups** section of the screen.
3. Select the backup that you know is safe.
4. Click the **Restore** button next to it.

The plugin will check you want to run the restore and it will then restore your site from that backup.

UNDER LOCK AND KEY: SITE SECURITY

OK, so now you know how important backups are.

But the chances are you'll never need to use one of those backups, as long as you keep your site secure.

WordPress is pretty secure out of the box (as long as you use a strong password), but there are things you can do to make it more secure. Read on to find out how to lock down your site so it's harder to bust into than Fort Knox.

BUSTING SOME MYTHS ABOUT SECURITY

First up, let's start with some myths.

WordPress used to have a reputation for being insecure. It was due to a number of factors, not least some dodgy plugins that have now been banished.

But the important thing is that if someone tells you not to get a WordPress website because WordPress is insecure, your answer to them should be: *not any more, it's not.* If they continue to argue, point out to them that some of the world's biggest and most tech-savvy brands have websites powered by WordPress.

Microsoft. Disney. The BBC. Facebook (not the Facebook platform itself, but their newsroom). The New York Times. And plenty more. These are companies that employ people who know a bit about internet security.

So you really needn't be worried about using WordPress.

So, let's move on to how you can make your site more secure. You can guarantee that those big brands are doing all this stuff (or their own variant of it), so why shouldn't you?

SECURITY SERVICES (NOT THE KIND YOU WRITE ABOUT)

Ooh, you're thinking. *I write spy novels. This is for me!*

Hmm. Maybe not. Unless you think that anyone would want to read a novel set in a company whose job is to monitor website uptime twenty-four hours a day.

No. I thought not.

What I'm talking about here are services you can sign up to that will help make your site more secure. Or to be more accurate, they will let you know when your site has been breached.

There are a few options available to you:

- If you're on WordPress.com, you get security baked in. There's no way the folks behind WordPress.com want a breach of your site affecting the rest of their network, so your site will be monitored and you'll be alerted if there's a problem. You can be confident no one can infiltrate the code in your site because if they infiltrated that, they'd have access to the entire network of millions of sites.
- With WordPress.org and Jetpack, use the monitoring that comes with the plugin. Jetpack will alert you if your site goes down and has a Protect feature that helps keep away brute force attacks. For enhanced security features, you'll need a premium WordPress.com plan—I think you're better off with a dedicated security plugin.
- If you're not using Jetpack, and want enhanced security features, you can install a dedicated security plugin.

These will help you add extra security to your site (so are worth installing even if you are using Jetpack), and you have the option of signing up for a premium service that will provide extra protection and support if your site does go down.

The plugin I use is Wordfence, which has a free version as well as a premium version with extra features and support.

INSTALLING AND CONFIGURING A SECURITY PLUGIN

Let's start by installing and activating the plugin via the plugins screen, in the normal way. If you worked through Chapter 15, you'll already have this plugin installed and have spent a little bit of time looking at it. Here we'll go into more detail.

Once the plugin is installed and activated, go to the **Wordfence** item that's appeared in your admin menu. This will take you to the dashboard.

You have two actions you can carry out: managing the firewall and running a scan. The plugin will automate scans for you regularly but as you've just installed the plugin, you might want to run a manual one.

Start by clicking on the option to manage the firewall. This will enhance protection for your site. Many of the options here are advanced or only available with the premium version of the plugin, but you can optimize the firewall with the free plugin. If you click the button for optimizing the firewall, you'll be prompted to download a backup of a file. Don't worry about the details of this: just keep working through the process, doing what the plugin tells you.

Once you've done that, click the **Back to dashboard** link at the top of the screen. There are more options you can configure but most of these work fine on their default settings. If you do need to tweak any of them in future (such as blocking specific search engines, for example), you can get advice from your hosting provider or check out the Wordfence documentation at wp4writers.com/wordfence.

Back on the dashboard, it's time to run a scan of your site. Click the **Manage Scan** button to go through to the scan management screen. Here you can configure the frequency of scans and how you're notified if there are problems. The defaults should be fine.

What we want to do here is run a scan. Click the **Start New Scan** button.

The plugin will then run a scan in the background. While it does this, you can continue working on your site.

Once it's done this, it'll give you information about any issues it's found. As all sites are different, I don't want to advise you on what you should do in response to the scan. Instead, follow the instructions and advice given by the plugin.

Sometimes it'll be easy to fix an issue raised by a scan, for example if you have plugins that need updating or a password that isn't secure enough. But sometimes you may have no control over the problem, because it's generated by the code inside a plugin.

If this does happen, you might want to consider whether you want to continue using that plugin. Wordfence will tell you how severe a risk the issue represents, and that will help you decide. If the issue is that a plugin hasn't been updated for compatibility with your version of WordPress, for example, it might not be a problem. But if the plugin contains dodgy code, you want to get rid of it. Go to the Plugins screen and deactivate it, then delete it. You may need to find an alternative plugin to do the same job first.

SECURE PASSWORDS

Your site is only as secure as the user credentials you use to access it.

If you install a security plugin like Wordfence, it will force you to use a secure password.

But even if you don't, you should use a password that is difficult to guess. This isn't just one that's tough for people to guess but one that's tough for a program designed to hack websites to guess. The chances are if your site is hacked, it'll be by one of those, not by a teenager sitting in his bedroom (he's busy hacking the Pentagon).

Here are some tips on secure passwords:

- Use a combination of upper and lower case letters.
- Add in some numbers and special characters (i.e. punctuation).
- Don't worry about using real words (bots aren't programed to run through the dictionary), but avoid using just one obvious word as your password—add some other characters to it.
- Don't use *admin* as the username for your administrator account. If you've already done this, you can't change it, but you can set up an alternative account and delete the first one.

How to set up a new admin account

Go to **Users > Add New**, add a new admin user with an email address you have access to (not that same one, WordPress won't let you do that), and save it.

Then log out of your admin account and log in to the new one. Go back to the Users screen and delete the old admin account. Now you can change the email address of your new account to the one you were using for the old accounts as there isn't a clash.

Using a secure password is so simple but it amazes me how few people do it. The most common user password in the world is *123456*. If you're using that, give yourself a rap on the knuckles, right now.

ADDING SSL TO YOUR SITE

Another way to make your site secure is by adding SSL, which stands for Secure Sockets Layer (I know, it doesn't help me understand what it is either). This will make your site's URL appear as *https://mysite.com* instead of *http://mysite.com*. It will make your site less vulnerable to attack and specifically to people scraping data from the front end.

If you're asking people to input personal information, but most especially if you're asking for credit card details, SSL is essential. It will also give you SEO benefits, as Google prefers sites with SSL. And it's free.

Go to cPanel on your hosting account and look for something called **Let's Encrypt**. This will be in the **Security** section of cPanel.

Select the domain name to which you want to add SSL and click the **Install** button. This will start the process of adding SSL to your site. You'll need to update this periodically which is a bit of a pain but it is free so you can't grumble too much. Before Let's Encrypt, I used to spend hundreds of dollars on SSL certificates each year, so don't complain!

What if my hosting provider doesn't provide Let's Encrypt?

The hosting providers I recommend (wp4writers.com/hosting) offer Let's Encrypt for free. But if your hosting provider doesn't include it as part of their plan, you have two options. You can buy SSL from your hosting provider for a charge, and they will install it for you. Or you can use the free WP Encrypt plugin.

This gives you a screen in the Settings menu that lets you generate a SSL certificate using Let's Encrypt. Simply go to the screen and enter the details of your site. For the country codes, refer to wp4writers.com/countrycodes. Then click the **Save Changes** button and the system will generate a certificate for you.

So that's security. The tips I've given you will help you to protect your site from attacks, as long as you also keep it up to date. Which leads me to...

37

KEEPING YOUR SITE SHINY AND NEW: UPDATES

I HAVE A CONFESSION.

In the previous chapter, on security, I missed out the thing you can do to have the biggest positive impact on your site's security.

And that's keeping your site updated.

I'm not talking about keeping your content updated: instead, I'm talking about the software. The themes and plugins you install, plus WordPress itself.

If you're on WordPress.com, you can crack a smug smile in the knowledge that this is all looked after for you. Skip this chapter and read on.

But if you're on WordPress.org, you'll need to either do this, or automate it. Let's look at why, and how.

WHY KEEP YOUR SITE UPDATED?

There are two main reasons for keeping your site up to date:

- It ensures you're using the latest, most up to date version of WordPress and your themes and plugins, with the benefits of any enhancements or new features.

- It ensures you have access to any security fixes.

Whenever a security vulnerability (or potential security vulnerability) is discovered with WordPress, or with a theme or plugin, the developers will quickly get to work to fix that vulnerability. They'll then release an update that contains that fix. These are called minor updates and they normally have a version number in the format *X.X.X.*

Major updates tend to introduce new features, and will have the format *X.X.*

WordPress will automatically run minor updates for you without you having to do anything. But it won't do that with major updates.

You can either turn on automation for major updates using a plugin, or you can run them yourself.

Let's start by looking at how you do it manually. (And when I say manually, I mean just clicking a button.)

STOP! BEFORE YOU UPDATE

Before you run an update, you should always take a backup of your site using your backup plugin. Sometimes an update might break your site, for example if your theme hasn't been tested with this version of WordPress and isn't compatible.

This isn't common, and has only happened to me with one plugin, the Yoast SEO plugin, which is why I don't recommend using it. But it's better to take that backup first (following the instructions in Chapter 35), to be on the safe side

Taken your backup? Good. Let's continue.

UPDATING WORDPRESS

To update WordPress, go to **Dashboard > Updates**.

If a new version of WordPress is available, you'll see a message telling you this. Click the button to update and wait for WordPress to do its thing.

That's all you need to do. No downloading of software, no editing code. You just click a button.

Once you've done the update, switch to the front end of your site (the screens your site visitors see), and test that everything's working as it should. If not, skip to the section below on *If an update breaks your site*.

Easy enough, but it's also easy to forget to do this. Which is why automation can be handy, more of which shortly.

UPDATING THEMES AND PLUGINS

Updating themes and plugins is equally simple.

You can either do this from the same Updates screen where you update WordPress, or from the Plugins screen or the Themes screen. It's up to you.

The Updates screen will give you a list of any themes or plugins that are out of date. Select them (or check the **Select All** box) and click the **Update Plugins** or **Update Themes** button. While the update is running, don't move away from the screen, or the update might fail. Just hold your horses and watch while your code updates —it won't take long. Or if you've got a bunch of plugins to update, go make yourself a coffee. You must be needing one by now.

If you're on the Plugins or Themes screen, you'll see a message underneath the name of the theme or plugin telling you if any of them are out of date. Just click the **Update** link below the theme or plugin's name and wait for WordPress to run the update. You can work your way down the screen updating all of the themes or plugins that need it, but don't leave the screen till they're all done.

AUTOMATING UPDATES

If you've installed a security plugin (and you should), then you'll get an email whenever you need to run an update. This way, you won't have to remember.

But you're a busy writer. You have literary masterpieces to drag out of your fevered brain. Wouldn't life be so much easier if you could skip the update process altogether, and have someone else do it for you?

Well, you can't quite do that. Not unless you have minions who are prepared to spend their time looking after your author website (thanks for buying my book, JK!). But you can do the next best thing, and that's to install a plugin that does updates for you automatically.

The plugin I recommend for this is the Easy Updates Manager plugin. It's free and you can install and activate it via the Plugins screen just like any other plugin.

Once you've done that, you may have a bit of a panic. You check the Settings menu and the Tools menu but there's nothing to be found. Where does this plugin keep its settings screen?

The answer is that it's sneaky, but also logical. You need to go to **Dashboard > Updates Options** to configure the plugin, because it lives in the same section of the admin menu as the Updates screen.

Go to that screen, then scroll down to configure which updates you want to automate. To make life as easy as possible for yourself, click the **Enable All Updates** button. If you want to have a bit more control, you can just automate WordPress core updates, or just plugin updates, or whatever you want.

You can also go the **Plugins** and/or **Themes** tabs to specify individual plugins and themes to automatically update. This is useful if you're running a theme or plugin that you know has occasionally broken your site after an update in the past.

Important: Backing up and automatic updates

If you set all updates to be automated, then you have no control over when updates will take place.

For this reason, I recommend you change the settings on your backup plugin so that your site is backed up every day. You might also want to increase the number of backups that are stored at any one time. If you don't visit your site until a week after a plugin has updated and then find it's broken the site, you want to be able to restore from a backup that was taken before the plugin was updated.

If you want backups to run automatically before an update, you can set Easy Updates Manager to do this, but you'll have to pay for the premium version of the plugin.

IF AN UPDATE BREAKS YOUR SITE (IT'S UNLIKELY)

Sometimes you'll run an update and it'll break something in your site.

This has happened to me a few times, and it's always been the fault of one plugin (I'm not going to repeat which).

As long as you only install plugins on your site that come from a reputable source (such as the WordPress theme or plugin directory, which is what you're accessing when you go to **Plugins > Add New** in your site), then this is very unlikely to happen. But I can't say it definitely won't. After all, the plugin that repeatedly broke my site (read the chapter on SEO to find out which) came from the plugin directory.

If it does, then it'll be for one of three reasons:

- One of your existing plugins or themes is incompatible with the new version of WordPress.
- One of your existing plugins or themes is incompatible with the new version of another plugin or theme.
- You've updated a plugin or theme and the new version has a bug.

It can be difficult to know which one is the culprit. You have two options.

Firstly, you can either restore the backup of the site you took before the update and then wait to run the backup until more updates are available. One of those updates might fix the problem, but it's difficult to know which or if it has.

Alternatively, you can try to diagnose the problem. Try these steps:

- If the problem comes after you update a plugin, try deactivating the plugin. Is the problem still there? If not, then it's probably the new version of the plugin that's to blame. Restore the backup of your site from before the update and wait for the plugin developer to release a new version of the plugin that fixes the problem. If they don't do this, you might want to find an alternative plugin that solves the problem.

- If the problem comes after a theme update, it could either be the fault of the theme or it may be compatibility between the theme and one of your plugins. Since you don't want to deactivate your theme (your site design would be lost if you did), you'll have to test your plugins instead. Try turning them off one by one and seeing if the problem persists. If it goes away, you've found your culprit. Either wait for a new version of the plugin to come out before updating the theme again, or find a new plugin.

- If the problem comes after a WordPress update, it's probably because one of your themes or plugins needs updating for compatibility with the new WordPress version. Start by testing your plugins in the way detailed above. If you find a culprit, it probably needs an update for compatibility. You can either disable the plugin until it's updated, or roll back your version of WordPress until the plugin is updated. I don't like running old versions of WordPress but if your plugin is essential for the smooth running of your site, this may be necessary.

- If the problem comes after a WordPress update and you can't find a plugin that's causing the problem, it may be your theme. Unless you're prepared to change your theme (a much more significant undertaking than with a

plugin), you'll have to roll back to the previous
WordPress version until the theme's updated.

If you don't have a backup from before a theme or plugin
update, you can always reinstall the older version of the theme or
plugin manually. Go to the Themes or Plugins screen and find the
theme or plugin. Click the **View details** link below the plug-
in/theme description. This will open a popup with the plug-
in/theme details.

On the right-hand side of the popup, click the link that says
WordPress.org Plugin/Theme Page. This will take you to the
page for the plugin or theme on the WordPress.org site. In the right-
hand sidebar, click the **Advanced View** link. Then scroll down to
the bottom of this page where you'll find a dropdown box with the
latest version number of the theme or plugin. Click on this and
select the second most recent version. Then click the **Download**
button.

This will download a zip file to your computer. Save it somewhere you can find it, and go back to your site. Click on the **Add
New** button at the top of the screen**.** Click the **Upload Plugin** or
Upload Theme button then select the zip file you just downloaded. Upload it, confirm you want it to replace the version of the
plugin/theme that's already on your site and activate it.

Phew! You now have the older version of the theme or plugin
installed. You'll see a notice in the Plugins or Themes screen telling
you it needs updating. Ignore it until another update is available that
fixes your problem.

38

HANG ON, SPEEDY: WEBSITE PERFORMANCE

SECURITY, backups, updates, will it ever end? I just want to get on with writing my blog, and maybe finishing this novel I've been working on if I get the time.

I know, I know. Site administration isn't the most exciting.

But luckily, this is all stuff you only have to do once. Set it up when you create your site, and you're set.

And this next section is about something you don't even need to set up immediately. If you decide to take a break for a few weeks and come back to this after you've finished your novel (yay! Well done you), then no one will berate you for it. Certainly not me.

But improving your site's speed (also referred to as performance) can bring you some benefits, and is worth spending some time on. It's not urgent—your site won't break if you don't do it. But it may get you more visitors, and it will certainly encourage them to stick around or come back again.

So let's start by looking at why site performance is worth taking the time to improve.

Note: this is all WordPress.org stuff. If you're on WordPress.com, you can't do anything to improve your site performance. Instead, those folks at WordPress.com are doing their best to make your site as fast as possible.

WHY SPEED IS IMPORTANT

There are two reasons why site speed is important.

The first is SEO. Google likes sites that run fast. When it crawls your site, one of the things it will measure is how long your pages (and that includes posts and archive pages) take to load. It will factor that in when deciding whether to show your site to people.

The second is visitor retention. Let's imagine someone finds a link to your author website in the back matter of your book (give yourself a brownie point for putting it there, not enough authors do). They type the link into their browser, and...

They wait.

And they wait.

And they wait a bit more.

And then they give up, and go back to looking at videos of funny cats (I mean, wouldn't you?).

You've lost them. They'll never try to access your site again.

That person might have joined your mailing list. They might have discovered your extensive backlist and followed the links to buy titles from it (please tell me you include that in your website). They might buy direct from you.

In short, you've missed out on an opportunity.

This is why speed is important. A fast site will get more visitors through SEO, and it won't lose visitors by taking too long to load.

THE IMPORTANCE OF QUALITY HOSTING

Now if your site is loading so slowly that it's making people give up before they even reach your site, it could be down to the content.

You could have uploaded a massive great image to your home page, and told WordPress to display it at full size. (If you're not sure how to fix this, check out Chapter 23.)

It could be a plugin that's slowing things down.

Or, and in most cases this is the prime culprit, it could be your hosting.

Some hosting providers offer deals that are so cheap they seem too good to be true. But you're on a budget, and they include one-click WordPress installation, so why not?

You sign up, pay your 50 cents a month (OK, so none are really quite that cheap), and you install WordPress. You get your site up and running (trying to ignore the fact that you spend more time waiting for the admin screens to load than actually doing anything), and you add some posts.

But then, when you go to your site, it's really slow.

You try it in a different browser. You go round to a friend's house to check it on their wifi. You try it on your phone.

But there's no getting away from it. Your site is slow.

If you buy rock-bottom hosting, you'll get a rock-bottom service.

But before you ditch your hosting provider and start all over again (see Chapter 19 for tips on migrating your site to a new WordPress installation—or even better, ask your new provider to do it for you, the good ones will), it's worth installing a performance plugin and running a few tests.

Just to be sure.

INSTALLING AND CONFIGURING A PERFORMANCE PLUGIN

There are a bunch of performance plugins out there, but the one I recommend is called Hummingbird. It's got a user-friendly interface and interacts with the Smush plugin that optimizes images—more of which shortly. Hummingbird is free—just install and activate it in the normal way.

Once you've activated the plugin, you'll find a Hummingbird item in your admin menu. Click on it and you'll see a popup prompting you to run a performance test. Click the button to run the test.

Hummingbird will then run the test and give you its results. For anything it thinks can be improved, it'll give you instructions and advice, or sometimes it'll simply provide you with a button you can click to fix things.

The actions you'll have to take will depend on the results of your test. Work through the screen that appears, reading the advice and taking any actions that you can. Sometimes you won't be able to do anything to fix some issues. For example, a speed test on my own site tells me that I'm not loading fonts in the best possible way. However, as I'm using Google fonts in my theme, there's nothing I can do to change this. I'm happy to live with this and move on to fixing issues I do have some control over.

There are some additional screens for this plugin that it's a good idea to use for extra performance enhancements. You'll find each of these in the Hummingbird menu item:

- **Caching**: this stores static HTML versions of your pages and posts, instead of loading them dynamically every time someone visits your site. When you edit a page or post, it generates a new, up-to-date version. Activate this to speed up page load times.
- **Gzip compression**: compressing files makes them quicker to load. Activate this for a bit more of a boost.
- **Asset optimization**: this will speed up loading of assets (i.e. files). You can also use the Smush plugin to optimize images.

IMPROVING IMAGE PERFORMANCE

As well as using the Hummingbird plugin to speed up your site, you can also use its sister plugin, Smush (it's actually called 'Smush Image Compression and Optimization', yikes), to make your images load faster.

The plugin will work through all of your images, working out how big they need to be to display correctly on your site. If it finds any that are too big, it will compress (or smush) them, so they load quicker.

Install and activate the plugin in the usual way, then click the

Smush link in the admin menu. Work though the setup screens, sticking with the defaults, then click the **Bulk Smush Now** button to smush all of your existing images.

You won't need to come back to this screen again, as the plugin will automatically smush all of your new images when you upload them. Saving you time and making your website run faster.

Note: Smush and Hummingbird are developed by the same company, and if you do decide you need the premium version of either of them, then you'll need to sign up for membership. This means you'll get the premium version of all of their plugins. They also have plugins for backups (Snapshot Pro) and security (Defender). They're one of my preferred providers of premium plugins, if you decide to go down the premium route. They have other great features including a hub you can use to monitor all of your websites if you have more than one.

WHEN THINGS GO WRONG

I HOPE you never have to read this chapter.

In fact, if you're treating this book like a novel and reading it from cover to cover, I encourage you to flip the page and move on. Nothing to see here, move along!

Because this chapter is designed to help you if you have a problem.

Here I've included information from elsewhere in the book (sometimes duplicated, sometimes new) that you can use as a reference if your site is hacked, or it breaks after an update, or anything else untoward happens.

So unless you're currently in a blind funk because your website isn't working and you don't know why, turn the page.

If you are in that blind funk, read on. I hope I can help you.

Note: This section is for WordPress.org users. If you're on WordPress.com and something goes wrong with your site, then you have two courses of action: undo that daft thing you just did, or contact the WordPress support team.

STEP 1: TRY NOT TO PANIC

Yes, I know you hate me for saying that. I know that the worst thing you can say to someone who's panicking is 'don't panic'.

But this is your author website.

It's not like you let the Olympic torch go out on your watch. Or lost an infinity stone. Or released a book full of the word *wibble* repeated over and over (I'd read it).

If your website goes down for a few hours, even for a day (heck, even for a week for most of us), it's not the end of the world.

Sit down. Get yourself a cup of your favorite hot beverage (sorry, you'll probably have to stand up again to do that). Pour a gin & tonic if you need it (not a large one, you need to focus). Take a few deep breaths.

I'm going to take you through a few steps: putting your site into maintenance mode, diagnosing the problem, and solving it.

Finished your breathing exercises? Drunk that cuppa? Got yourself another one?

Great. Here goes.

STEP 2: MAINTENANCE MODE

If your site is doing something horrible, you don't want the world to see it. So let's put it into maintenance mode.

You can only do this if you have access to your site. If you don't, skip forward to the diagnosis section, then come back once you have access to the WordPress admin screens.

Install and activate the Coming Soon plugin (full title: 'Coming Soon Page & Maintenance Mode by SeedProd', boy I hate long plugin titles).

You'll get a new menu item in the admin menu (yes, another one, the days when plugins were happy to put their screens in the Settings menu seem to be long gone). It's called **SeedProd** (intuitive, I know). If you aren't taken to the settings screen for the plugin when you activate it, click this link to go to it.

Scroll down to the **Page Settings** section. Add some text telling visitors that your site is currently unavailable because of scheduled maintenance (they don't need to know what's really going on). Have some fun with the text if you like, if your panicked brain can handle it. Maybe a message in the form of a story? OK, maybe not.

Click the **Save All Changes** button. Then click the **Preview** tab to see what your maintenance screen looks like. If you want, tweak the colors and add your logo or photo via the **Design** tab. Or not, if you're in a hurry or your brain is refusing to function.

Now, back on the **Content** tab, select the **Enable Maintenance Mode** radio button and click the **Save All Changes** button.

Phew! You can still see your broken site but other people can't. Now if you have other things to do before fixing your site, you can go away and do them. If you want to fix your site immediately, read on.

STEP 3: DIAGNOSIS AND SOLUTION

I'm including the next steps (diagnosis and solution) together because one will depend on the other. In other words, your solution will depend on your diagnosis.

So let's work out what the problem is. Work your way through the questions below, in order.

DOES YOUR SITE STILL LOOK LIKE YOUR SITE BUT A BROKEN VERSION OF IT?

In other words, is your WordPress installation still running your site?

If so, skip to the next question.

If not, your site will look completely different from how it should. It might be like the time my site was hacked (on a camping holiday, yes you've read that story). It had a black screen, yellow text in Arabic and odd mwahaha-style music. Nothing like my real site.

This means there are files running your site that aren't part of your WordPress installation. And unless you're happy editing the files in your site, it's one your hosting provider can help you fix.

Raise an urgent support ticket and ask them to help. They should be motivated to help you: after all, a security breach on their server is something they should take seriously.

If your hosting provider refuses to help, you may need to switch providers. Take your backup and install it on a new site (see below). A headache, I know, but this is the most extreme course of action and something very few people need to do.

Alternatively, you may be able to hire an expert to help you fix it. Ask around for recommended WordPress security experts or just ask your developer if you already have one.

DID YOU JUST PUBLISH OR EDIT A POST OR PAGE OR CHANGE A SETTING?

Try undoing what you just did. You may have made an error, and undoing it could fix the problem.

Still not working? Move on to the next question.

HAVE YOU JUST RUN AN UPDATE?

If so, the problem will be either with the new version of WordPress, a new version of a theme or plugin, or incompatibility between that and something else on your site.

Flick to Chapter 37 and follow the instructions in the *If an Update Breaks Your Site (It's Unlikely)* section.

If you haven't recently run an update (and that needn't mean just now, it could be any time since you last checked the site, and it could have been an automatic update), keep reading.

HAVE YOU RECEIVED A NOTIFICATION FROM YOUR SECURITY PLUGIN?

Check your emails. If there's nothing there, check the admin screen for the security plugin.

Are there any warnings? If so, follow the instructions given.

Work though any warnings, instructions or advice then check your site again. If it works, you're all set. If not, keep going.

YOU'RE GOING TO NEED HELP

If you have access to WordPress, haven't run an update, and have no warnings from your security plugin, then it's going to be difficult for you to diagnose the problem.

Your hosting provider has access to more information than you, however, and should be able to help. Raise a support ticket, explaining what's happening, and ask if they can help.

Important: before you do this, take a backup. Your hosting provider may need to edit some of your files and you want a backup in case this causes more problems (even hosting support teams aren't infallible). Make sure you don't overwrite any earlier backups.

IF YOUR HOSTING PROVIDER CAN'T (OR WON'T) HELP

If your hosting provider isn't able to help, you'll need to restore your site from the last backup that you know works correctly.

Assuming you're using the UpdraftPlus plugin, follow these steps:

1. Go to **Settings > UpdraftPlus Backups**.
2. Scroll down to the **Existing Backups** section of the screen.
3. Select the backup that you know is safe.
4. Click the **Restore** button next to it.

The plugin will check you want to run the restore and it will then restore your site from that backup.

WHEN ALL ELSE FAILS

In over 99% of cases, things will be working now.

If not, you might need to move to a clean WordPress installation, maybe with a new hosting provider.

If you're happy with your hosting provider, you can install a new WordPress installation and migrate your site to that.

If you haven't been happy with your hosting provider, or suspect the problem may be their fault, you'll need to start again with a new hosting provider.

Below I'll give you two sets of steps. Follow the first set if you plan to stay with your existing hosting provider, and the second if you want to move.

Steps if you're staying with your hosting provider:

1. Ask if your hosting provider will create a clean WordPress installation for you and migrate your site across to it. If they will (and it works), that's great—no more work for you. Make sure they know your site is broken so they don't migrate any problems across. If they won't do this, move on to step 2.
2. Make a note of all the themes and plugins you have installed on your site.
3. Make a backup of your site and make sure you have a copy of the files stored somewhere other than your server (e.g. Google Drive or your computer). I recommend also using the Export tool (see Chapter 19) to export your posts and pages, just in case you can't restore the backup. Alternatively, make sure you have a backup from when your site was last working.
4. Go to cPanel and find the WordPress auto-installer. Use it to delete your existing WordPress installation (scary, I

know). Now use it again to add a new WordPress installation.

5. Install all the same themes and plugins in your new site that you had in your old site. Don't worry about configuring them—the restore from your backup will do that.

6. In UpdraftPlus, go to **Settings > UpdraftPlus Backups**. Scroll down to the **Existing Backups** section of the screen. Select the backup that you know is safe and click the **Restore** button next to it.

7. If you can't get the restore to work, use the Import tool (see Chapter 19) to import your content. You'll need to install your theme and all your plugins and configure them first, as the importer doesn't copy those. Laborious, but it will be working it.

Now your site should be working. If it's not, and your hosting provider still won't help, the only resort is to switch hosting providers.

Steps for switching hosting providers:

1. If you're switching hosting providers, find one who will do the migration for you. Let them have a copy of your backup files or access to your old site (don't delete it yet).

2. They might tell you that your backup files are corrupted or that they can't migrate the site because it's broken. In this case, you'll need to set up a new WordPress installation with them and create your site following steps 5 & 6 above.

3. Once the site has migrated across, ask your new hosting provider to migrate the domain name. This will take a few days to take effect but once it's done, you'll be all set.

Phew! Either way, you will now have a working site. If you do switch hosting providers, this is an opportunity to find one who will bend over backwards to help you get your site working properly. In my experience, hosting providers are generally very helpful in this situation, as they are keen to take your business from a rival. Shop around and find someone who will make the process as easy as possible for you.

X

OVER TO YOU

40

A WEBSITE IS FOR LIFE, NOT JUST FOR CHRISTMAS

Woot!

You now have an author website, congratulations!

Whether you chose to use WordPress.com or WordPress.org (or WordPress.org with a hint of WordPress.com, thanks to the Jetpack plugin), I hope this book has helped you to work through the process of creating your website and making it work in the way you need it to. I also hope it helps you find more fans and sell more books.

But before we go, I want to leave you with a dull but important message, and that's that a website is never 'done.'

Your website is something that will evolve and grow over time. You'll add more content to it, you'll add new plugins and new features, and you'll make tweaks to the design from time to time.

If your website is going to be as effective as possible, you need to maintain it. And that means:

- Adding new posts regularly to keep your readers updated and draw in more readers via SEO.
- Updating your Books page every time you have a new book out.
- Making sure your About Me page is kept up to date (if it

says you're working on your first novel, you'll need to update that when you move on to your second).

- Keep your plugins and themes and WordPress itself updated.
- Make sure your site is getting backed up regularly.
- Respond to any security warnings you get from your security plugin and fix any problems.
- Finally, and importantly, find ways of driving traffic to your site: your books' back matter, your social media accounts, adverts and anything else you can use.

If you do all this, you'll have a website that supports your career as an author and forms the hub of your author platform. Good luck!

EXTRA RESOURCES

There are loads of tutorials, guides and snippets of advice on my website rachelmcwrites.com. I send out a weekly newsletter that includes tips on author websites and other writing-related topics. You can sign up for that and get a free copy of my book *Author Website Blueprint* at rachelmcwrites.com/blueprint. Stay in touch, I'd love to hear from you!

JARGON BUSTER

THIS BOOK IS full of jargon—no getting away from it.

I normally hate jargon, but find it impossible to write a book about a technical subject like this with dipping into it from time to time.

So instead of flinging the book at the wall because it's full of gobbledygook, I hope that you can get the definitions and clarification you need from this jargon buster.

If you can't, please let me know. You can email me at rachel@rachelmcwrites.com or follow me on Facebook or Twitter as rachelmcwrites, and ask for clarification there.

If you ask me to translate some jargon that's in this book but not in the jargon buster, I can add it in a later edition of the book. Hopefully I won't have to do that, as you'll find your answers here.

Right! Preamble over with. Here's the jargon buster in all its glory.

DOMAIN NAME

A domain name is the address someone types into their browser to access your website. For example I have *rachelmcwrites.com* for my nonfiction website.

Every website has to have a domain name, so that people can find it. So if you're on WordPress.com, you'll have a domain name that includes *wordpress.com*—e.g. *rachelmcwrites.wordpress.com*. That bit at the beginning before the period is called a subdomain.

You can choose to use your own domain name with Word-Press.com for a fee—see Chapter 8.

For a self-hosted site, you need to register a domain name with a domain registrar and pay a small amount (up to $10 a year). Alternatively lots of hosting providers will give you a domain name as part of your website package.

Note that when you see your domain name in the browser, it'll have *http://* or *https://* in front of it. This is just a way of indicating that it's on the internet. The *https://* is more secure and means the website has SSL. Most websites don't bother using *www* anymore.

URL

URL stands for uniform resource locator.

No, that doesn't help you at all, does it?

A URL is the address of an individual page on the internet, not just the website it's on. So my books page on *rachelmcwrites.com* would be *rachelmcwrites.com/books*.

The URL consists of two things: the domain name (*rachelmcwrites.com*), and the slug for that page(*books*), with a forward slash in between. WordPress defines the slug for you based on the title of the page or post, and you can edit it if you want something specific.

SSL

SSL stands for Secure Sockets Layer (another acronym that's not the slightest bit helpful). If your website has an SSL certificate, it will appear with *https://* instead of *http://* in front of the domain name.

Websites with SSL are more secure and will also rank higher with search engines, as Google likes security.

Find out how to get SSL in Chapter 36.

WEBSITE HOSTING

If you have a self-hosted WordPress site, then that site needs to sit on a server somewhere, just like every other site on the internet.

To make this possible, you pay for hosting from a company known as a hosting provider. For a monthly (sometimes annual) fee, they will rent you server space where you can host your website.

The hosting company doesn't own your site, any more than a hotel owns the clothes you put in the closet when you rent a room. But, just like a hotel, it does have rules about what it'll allow on its turf. So you won't be able host illegal activity on your website or use your hosting account to store anything other than a website.

CONTENT MANAGEMENT SYSTEM (CMS)

A CMS is a system that lets you create a website without writing any code. The world's most popular CMS is WordPress.

WordPress (like most content management systems) consists of three things:

- The software itself that runs the CMS (WordPress includes a bunch of files to make it run).
- The files you add to make your site unique. With WordPress.org, these will be the themes and plugins you install plus any media you upload. With WordPress.com, these are the themes and plugins provided by the platform, plus your media.
- A database, which stores all of your content (i.e. your posts and pages) and settings.

WordPress.com and WordPress.org both use the same software: the difference is where it's hosted.

WEBSITE BUILDER

A system designed to let you create website without writing code, often with a drag-and-drop interface.

Website builders are often built on a similar framework as a CMS, but will be less effective for blogging and regular content creation. They can also be quite expensive and are a lot less flexible.

SEARCH ENGINE OPTIMIZATION (SEO)

SEO is what you do to enhance the chances of your site (or an individual post or page) being found by search engines and placed high in the rankings for a particular search term.

You can enhance your SEO by using a robust website system like WordPress; by making your site run fast; by writing quality content; and by using an SEO plugin.

MAILING LIST / NEWSLETTER

An author newsletter is a regular email you send out to readers who subscribe to your mailing list, giving you their email address so you can keep in touch with them.

To set up a mailing list, you'll need to use a mailing list provider like MailChimp or MailerLite. This is more robust and reliable than simply sending emails from your own email account, which are likely not to be delivered if you send them in bulk.

If you're setting up a mailing list, there are rules on what you can do with people's email addresses and how you can store them. Another good reason to use a mailing list provider, as the data is kept securely.

FRONT END

The front end of your website is the public website that visitors see. This is different from the admin, or back end, which you use to manage the site and add content.

WORDPRESS ADMIN / BACK END / DASHBOARD

The WordPress admin is the set of screens you use to manage your website and add content to it.

The dashboard is strictly speaking just the one screen called Dashboard, but it's often used to refer to all the admin screens.

Depending on whether you're with WordPress.com or Word-Press.org, you'll have a different set of admin screens. Over time it's likely that the WordPress.org screens will look more and more like the ones from WordPress.com.

PLUGIN

A plugin is extra code that makes something happen on your site. It might add a link to your newsletter provider, or an online store, or a gallery of cute cat photos. It means that the core code for Word-Press itself doesn't have to include stuff you might not need. If you want that extra functionality, just install a plugin.

Installing plugins is easy and you can do it from the WordPress admin screens. I cover it in Chapter 15.

WIDGETS / SIDEBARS / WIDGET AREAS

A widget is a snippet of content or code that you can add to every page in your site. Examples are lists of posts, social media feeds and newsletter signup forms. These aren't part of any post, but sit outside it in a widget area.

A widget area is an area on the pages in your site where you can place widgets. The widget areas are defined in your theme, and may be in a sidebar (next to the content) or the footer (below the content). Some themes even have widget areas in the header or on the home page.

A sidebar is an area of space in your page which is to the side of the main content. Sometimes you'll hear sidebars and widget areas referred to interchangeably, but they aren't the same thing. Your sidebar is probably just one of the widget areas in your site.

CUSTOM POST TYPE

WordPress comes with a bunch of post types that you can use without having to activate any extra features. These are posts, pages and attachments (i.e. media). With WordPress.org, you can add as many extra post types as you want, and these are called custom post types. For example, you would create a 'product' post type if you're adding a store to your site.

With WordPress.com you can't add your own post types, but you can activate testimonials and/or portfolios if you want.

PAGES AND POSTS

A page is static content that doesn't change over time, such as your contact page or your 'About me' page. A post is an update, or a blog post.

Most of the content you'll be creating will be posts. Posts are listed on your blog page and they're what you'll be sharing with your audience and using to keep your site fresh.

Sometimes in this book, you'll see me referring to a web page more generically: this is any type of page in your site, including a static page, a post, or an archive page (e.g. the list of posts on a category).

AUTHOR WEBSITE BLUEPRINT

Do you know you need an author website but have no idea how to go about creating one? Websites can be daunting but this guide aims to make things simple. Learn how to:

- Decide which website platform to use
- Design your site so it fits with your book covers
- Add content to your site and use it to engage readers
- Add newsletter signups to your site
- Sell books direct to readers.

With a useful resources section and lots of actionable tips you can use today.

Get your FREE copy at rachelmcwrites.com/blueprint.

THE NOVEL PLANNING WORKBOOK

Everyone's got a novel in them…

But how do you go from initial story idea to finished novel?

This workbook will help you plan your novel and go from blank page to novel outline, is you can start writing.

It's designed as a resource for you to use to make your notes and plan your story, with sections for:

Plan Your Book - From Blank Page to Outlined Novel

RACHEL McCOLLIN

- Identifying your story premise.
- Sketching your characters.
- Identifying theme.
- Working out the major plot points.
- Weaving in subplots and minor characters.

The Novel Planning Workbook will help you plot your novel and turn you from a wannabe writer to a novelist.

ACKNOWLEDGMENTS

This is the page that you either miss out or you trawl through with a fine tooth comb to see if you're mentioned. So I'll keep it brief.

The following people helped make this book a thing.

People who taught me about WordPress and showed me that you can never know enough about the subject: Mike Little, Tom McFarlin, Jonny Allbut and Mark Wilkinson.

The editor who helped hone my technical writing skills and gave me lots of encouragement: Raelene Morey.

My lovely beta readers who road tested the book and told me what worked and what was broken: Heide Goody, Jane Andrews.

And the person who suggested I put the website advice I was giving out at conferences into a book: Justin Anderson. Thanks for giving me a shedload more work (you know I don't mean it).

www.ingramcontent.com/pod-product-compliance
Lightning Source LLC
LaVergne TN
LVHW022302060326
832902LV00020B/3223